LEARNING ORGANIZATIONAL CHANGING STRATEGIES

JOHN LOK

Copyright © John Lok
All Rights Reserved.

This book has been published with all efforts taken to make the material error-free after the consent of the author. However, the author and the publisher do not assume and hereby disclaim any liability to any party for any loss, damage, or disruption caused by errors or omissions, whether such errors or omissions result from negligence, accident, or any other cause.

While every effort has been made to avoid any mistake or omission, this publication is being sold on the condition and understanding that neither the author nor the publishers or printers would be liable in any manner to any person by reason of any mistake or omission in this publication or for any action taken or omitted to be taken or advice rendered or accepted on the basis of this work. For any defect in printing or binding the publishers will be liable only to replace the defective copy by another copy of this work then available.

Contents

Preface

Introduction

Management science is a popular business, economic and psychological method to be applied to help any business organizations, societies to solve problems. Whether what are the real functions or advantages that management science methods or strategies can help our societies or organizations to solve any problems ? Why and how social changing environment may influence organizational strategies need to be changed?

Prologue

brings employees efficiencies
● Predictive the choosing right
data asset and (FM) analytics
solutions to boost public
transportation service quality
● The relationship between facility
management and productive
efficiency
   ● The relationship between facility
management and consumer
behavior
   ● Facility management influences
consumer satisfactory service
feeling
   ● Facility management how influences
employee Psychology to raise
productive efficiency

● How to impact of workplace
management on well-being and
productivity
   ● Facility management technological
factor how influences workers
performance in construction industry
   ● How organizational facility environment
factor influences new and old employees
long term performance p.41-60
   Reference
   Chapter 4
Why social behavior may influence organizational strategy needs to be
changed

Human Behavioral network job brings social
economic benefits
   What does human network job mean
   Why human network job behavior may influence economy

Robots take our jobs behavioral and economy influences

Robot job behavior brings economy influences

Intellectual human economic behaviors
What does intellectual human economic behaviors
mean ?
The relationship between social change and human
behavior
How human productive behavior may influence economic development

● New Zealand farmer individual wine productive behavior
● America high technological productive behavior
● China share market investing behavior
Why has any individual country have many people invest share behavior
which can influence the country's macro consumption desire?
Can technology influence human shopping behavioral change?
Why and how human behavior may influence the country's economic
growth or recession?
Technology how impacts human behavior changing?
How and why employees behaviors may influence economy development?
Robots invention whether they can help organizations to raise efficiencies
or inefficiencies?
Why social behavior may influence organizational strategy needs to be
changed ? p.61-90

CHAPTER ONE

INTRODUCTION OF MANAGEMENT SCIENCE

Management Science (MS) can be defined as:

In micro solution level view, "A problem-solving process used by an interdisciplinary team to develop mathematical models that represent simple-to-complex functional relationships and provide management with a basis for decision-making and a means of uncovering new problems for quantitative analysis

Management science encompasses, however, more than just the development of models for specific problems. It makes a substantial contribution in a much broader area: the application of the output from management science models for decision-making at the lower, middle, and top management levels.

A manager's experience, upcoming business conditions, and the output from a mathematical model form the best combination for planning, organizing, directing and controlling the company's activities. Management science is the application of the scientific method to the study of the operations of large, complex organisations or activities. Two disciplines intimately associated with management science are industrial engineering and operations research.

Definition and Concept of Management Science:

In macro solution view, management science (MS) is the broad interdisciplinary study of problem solving and decision making in human organizations, with strong links to management, economics, business, engineering, management consulting, and other fields. It uses various scientific research-based principles, strategies, and analytical methods including mathematical modeling, statistics and numerical algorithms to improve an organization's ability to enact rational and accurate management decisions by arriving at optimal or near optimal solutions to complex decision problems. Management science helps businesses to achieve goals using various scientific methods.

The field was initially an outgrowth of applied mathematics, where early challenges were problems relating to the optimization of systems which could be modeled linearly, i.e., determining the optima (maximum value of profit, assembly line performance, crop yield, bandwidth, etc. or minimum of loss, risk, costs, etc.) of some objective function. Today, management science encompasses any organizational activity for which the problem can be structured as a functional system so as to obtain a solution set with identifiable characteristics.

Management science is concerned with a number of different areas of study: One is developing and applying models and concepts that may prove useful in helping to illuminate management issues and solve managerial problems. The models used can often be represented mathematically, but sometimes computer-based, visual or verbal representations are used as well or instead. Another area is designing and developing new and better models of organizational excellence.

Management science research can be done on three levels:
The fundamental level lies in three mathematical disciplines: probability, optimization, and dynamical systems theory.
The modeling level is about building models, analyzing them mathematically, gathering and analyzing data, implementing models on computers, solving them, experimenting with them—all this is part of management science research on the modeling level. This level is mainly instrumental, and driven mainly by statistics and econometrics.
The application level, just as in any other engineering and economics disciplines, strives to make a practical impact and be a driver for change in the real world.
The management scientist's mandate is to use rational, systematic, science-based techniques to inform and improve decisions of all kinds. The techniques of management science are not restricted to business applications but may be applied to military, medical, public administration,

charitable groups, political groups or community groups.

Historical Development of Management Science:
The roots of management science extend to the work of F.W. Taylor, the father of Scientific Management. Taylor is known for his systematic development of management techniques which he started at the Midvale Steel Company in Philadelphia around 1880.
(i) Research,
    (ii) Standardization,
    (iii) Control and
    (iv) Cooperation.

When installed at the Link Belt Engineering Company in 1905, the system included cost accounting, time study, inventory control, production control, planning, output scheduling, functional operation, standardized procedures, a mnemonic system of classification, and means for maintaining quality production. Associated with Taylor were other important pioneers of scientific management – Carl Barth, Gantt, Thompson, Hathaway and many others. Barth brought to the work of scientific management the use of research mathematics, which he merged with his extensive knowledge of machine tools. Gantt contributed the recognition of worker psychology, the development of a bonus plan, and the charts used in production scheduling. Out of this came the term Industrial Engineering which today is descriptive of the work of functional staffs responsible for such activities as incentive standards, methods analysis, quality control, production control, cost control and materials handling.
During the ten years just after World War II, a great deal of management science was performed under the name of operations research. The influx of physical scientists many of whom were unacquainted with modern management administration into war technology and the pressures of total war with new and terrible weapons gave rise to a rediscovery of a kind of pragmatic scientific management. This merged with an increasingly popular acceptance of statistical quality control in America and the practical development of high-speed electronic calculators to give impetus to the operations-research approach.
In brief, management science describes an integrated approach to operational control based on the application of scientific research methods to business problems. A systematic approach to problem solving received early impetus from Taylor's scientific management movement and is

continued today by Industrial engineers and mathematical business analysts. This approach is characterized by a methodology of sequential investigation steps.

Characteristics of Management Science:

The four major characteristics of management science are as follows:-

(1) Examine Functional Relationships from a Systems Overview:

The activity of any one function of a company will have some effect on the activity of each of the other functions. Therefore it is necessary to identify all important interactions and determine their impact on the company as a whole. Initially, the functional relationships in a management science project are expanded deliberately so that all the significantly interacting parts and their related components are contained in a statement of the problem. A systems overview examines the entire area under the manager's control. This approach provides a basis for initiating inquiries into problems that seem to be affecting performance at all levels.

2) Use the Interdisciplinary Approach:

Management science makes good use of a simple principle, it looks at the problem from different angles and approaches. For example, a mathematician might look at the inventory problem and formulate some type of mathematical relationships between the manufacturing departments and customer demand. A chemical engineer might look at the same problem and formulate it in terms of flow theory. A cost accountant might conceive the inventory problem in terms of component costs (e.g., direct material cost, direct labour cost, overheads etc.) and how such costs can be controlled and reduced, etc. Therefore, management science emphasizes over the interdisciplinary approach because each of the individual aspects of a problem can be best understood and solved by those, experts in different fields such as accounting, biological, economic, engineering, mathematics, physical, psychological, sociological, statistical etc.

(3) Uncover New Problems for Study:

The third characteristic of management science, which is often overlooked, is that the solution of an MS problem brings new problems to light. All interrelated problems uncovered by the MS approach do not have to be solved at the same time. However, each must be solved with consideration for other problems if maximum benefits are to be obtained.

(4) Use a Modeling-Process Approach to Problem Solving:

Management science takes a systematic approach to problem solving. It may use a modeling process approach taking the help of mathematical models.

Other Characteristics of Management Science are:

(5) A primary focus on managerial decision-making.

(6) The application of science to decision-making.

(7) A dependence on electronic computers.

(8) An appraisal resting on criteria of economic effectiveness. Effectiveness may be defined as the extent to which goals are achieved. Effectiveness is evaluated by measures of effectiveness (also known as measures of performance).

The Tools of Management Science:

The tools of management science developed specifically for solving managerial problems are listed below:

(a) Decision Matrices:

Allocation and investment problems involving a relatively small number of possible solutions can be presented in a tabular form known as decision matrix.

(b) Decision Trees:

The extension of decision matrices for situations involving several decision periods takes the shape of a tree.

(c) Mathematical Programming:

It attempts to maximize the attainment level of one goal subject to a set of requirements and limitations. It has extensive use in business, economics, engineering, the military and public service, mainly as an aid to the solution of allocation problems.

(d) Branch and Bound:

It is a step-by-step procedure used when a very large (or even infinite) number of alternatives exist for certain managerial problems.

(e) Network Models:

This is a family of tools designed for the purpose of planning and controlling complex projects. The best known models are PERT and CPM.

(f) Dynamic Programming:

It is an approach to decisions that are basically sequential in nature or can be reformulated so as to be considered sequential. It is a very general and powerful tool.

(g) Markov Chains:

They are used for predicting the outcome of processes where systems or units change their condition over time (e.g., consumers change their preferences for certain brands of commodities).

(h) Game Theory:

It provides a systematic approach to decision-making in competitive environments and a framework for the study of conflict.

(i) Inventory Models:

For certain types of inventory control problems, certain models that attempt to minimize the cost associated with ordering and carrying inventories have been developed.

(j) Waiting Line (Queuing) Models:

For certain types of problems involving queues, special descriptive models have been developed to predict the performance of service systems such as car garages – cars standing in queue for servicing.

(k) Simulation Models:

For the analysis of complex systems when all other models fail, management science uses descriptive-type simulation models.

Specially, five types of models may be employed:

1. Artificial Intelligence.
2. Heuristic programming.
3. Management games.
4. Systems simulation, and
5. Monte Carlo simulation.

APPLY MANAGEMENT SCIENCE METHODS TO SOLVE PROBLEMS STEPS:

Step 1 : Searching or finding what is/are the main problem(s)

We first present a working definition of science. We use that definition along with our review of evidence on compliance with science by papers published in leading journals to develop operational guidelines for implementing scientific principles. We then developed a checklist to help researchers follow the guidelines, and another to help reviewers—those who fund, publish, or use research to assess whether a paper complies with scientific principles.

While the scientific principles underlying our guidelines are well-established, our presentation of them in the form of comprehensive checklists of operational guidance for science is novel. We present evidence that in the absence of such an aid, researchers and research stakeholders will often fail to observe scientific principles. Giving specific and realistic suggestions for addressing our society's pervasive social problems .

Updated with recent issues such as the national debate on health care reform, this Second Edition of How Can We Solve Our Social Problems? gives students a sense of hope by demonstrating specific, realistic steps we can take to solve some of the most pervasive social problems in America today. Author James Crone maintains a sense of sociological objectivity throughout and helps students realize that we can take steps to solve such key social problems as poverty, racial and ethnic inequality, unequal education, and environmental issues. The book's first two chapters define "social problem,," provide a theoretical background, discuss the daunting barriers we face in attempting to solve social problems, and demonstrate how sociology can help.

Research question: Can managers apply management science to solve social problem ?

Problem: The scientific method is unrivalled as a basis for generating useful knowledge, research papers published in the management and social sciences and applied economics fields often violate scientific principles. What can be done to to increase the publication of useful papers?

Methods: Evidence on researchers' compliance with scientific principles was examined. Guidelines aimed at reducing violations were then derived from established definitions of the scientific method.

Guidelines to Problem Solving and DecisionMaking (Rational Approach) Much of what people do is solve problems and make decisions. Often, stressed and very short for time. Consequently, when they encounter a new problem or decision they must make, they react with a decision that seemed to work before. It's easy with this approach to get stuck in a circle of solving the same problem over and over again. Therefore, it's often useful to get used to an organized approach to problem solving and decision making. Not all problems can be solved and decisions made by the following, rather rational approach. (Note that it might be more your nature to view a "problem" as an"opportunity". Therefore, you might substitute "problem"for "opportunity" in the following guidelines.)

Step 2: Define the problem

This is often where people struggle. They react to what they think the problem is. Instead, seek to understand more about why you think there's a problem.

Define the problem: (with input from yourself and others). Ask yourself andothers, the following questions:

1. What can you see that causes you to think there's a problem?

2. Where is it happening?

3. How is it happening?

4. When is it happening?

5. With whom is it happening? (HINT: Don't jump to "Who is causing theproblem?" When we're stressed, blaming is often one of our first reactions.To be an effective manager, you need to address issues more than people.)

6. Why is it happening?

7. Write down a five-sentence description of the problem in terms of "Thefollowing should be happening, but isn't ..." or "The followingis happening and should be: ..." As much as possible, be specific inyour description, including what is happening, where, how, with whom and why.(It may be helpful at this point to use a variety of research methods.

Step 3: Defining complex problems

If the problem still seems overwhelming, break it down by repeating steps 1-7 until you have descriptions of several related problems. Verifying your understanding of the problems: It helps a great deal to verify your problem analysis for conferring with apeer or someone else.

Step 4: Prioritize the problems

If you discover that you are looking at several related problems, then prioritizewhich ones you should address first. Note the difference between "important" and "urgent" problems.Often, what we consider to be important problems to consider are really justurgent problems. Important problems deserve more attention. For example, ifyou're continually answering "urgent" phone calls, then you've probablygot a more "important" problem and that's to design a system thatscreens and prioritizes your phone calls.

Step 5: Understand your role in the problem

Your role in the problem can greatly influence how you perceive the role ofothers. For example, if you're very stressed out, it'll probably look like othersare, too, or, you may resort too quickly to blaming and reprimanding others.Or, you are feel very guilty about your role in the problem, you may ignorethe accountabilities of others.

Step 6: Look at potential causes for the problem

• It's amazing how much you don't know about what you don't know.

Therefore,in this phase, it's critical to get input from other people who notice theproblem and who are effected by it.

• It's often useful to collect input from other individuals one at a time(at least at first). Otherwise, people tend to be inhibited about offeringtheir impressions of the real causes of problems.

• Write down what your opinions and what you've heard from others.

• Regarding what you think might be performance problems associated withan employee, it's often useful to seek advice from a peer or your supervisorin order to verify your impression of the problem.

• Write down a description of the cause of the problem and in terms of whatis happening, where, when, how, with whom and why.

Step 7: Identify alternatives for approaches to resolve the problem

At this point, it's useful to keep others involved (unless you're facing apersonal and/or employee performance problem). Brainstorm for solutions to theproblem. Very simply put, brainstorming is collecting as many ideas as possible,then screening them to find the best idea. It's critical when collecting theideas to not pass any judgment on the ideas -- just write them down as you hearthem. (A wonderful set of skills used to identify the underlying cause of issuesis Systems Thinking.)

Step 8: Select an approach to resolve the problem

•When selecting the best approach, consider:

• Which approach is the most likely to solve the problem for the long term?

• Which approach is the most realistic to accomplish for now? Do you havethe resources? Are they affordable? Do you have enough time to implement theapproach?

• What is the extent of risk associated with each alternative?

   (The nature of this step, in particular, in the problem solving process iswhy problem solving and decision making are highly integrated.)

Step 9: Plan the implementation of the best alternative (this is your action plan)

1.Carefully consider "What will the situation look like when the problemis solved?"

2. What steps should be taken to implement the best alternative to solvingthe problem? What systems or processes should be changed in your organization,for example, a new policy or procedure? Don't resort to

solutions where someoneis "just going to try harder".

3. How will you know if the steps are being followed or not? (these are yourindicators of the success of your plan)

4. What resources will you need in terms of people, money and facilities?

5. How much time will you need to implement the solution? Write a schedulethat includes the start and stop times, and when you expect to see certainindicators of success.

6. Who will primarily be responsible for ensuring implementation of the plan?

7. Write down the answers to the above questions and consider this as youraction plan.

8. Communicate the plan to those who will involved in implementing it and,at least, to your immediate supervisor.

(An important aspect of this step in the problem-solving process is continuallyobservation and feedback.)

Step 10: Monitor implementation of the plan

Monitor the indicators of success:

1. Are you seeing what you would expect from the indicators?

2. Will the plan be done according to schedule?

3. If the plan is not being followed as expected, then consider: Was the planrealistic? Are there sufficient resources to accomplish the plan on schedule?Should more priority be placed on various aspects of the plan? Should theplan be changed?

Step 11: Verify if the problem has been resolved or not

One of the best ways to verify if a problem has been solved or not is to resumenormal operations in the organization. Still, you should consider:

1. What changes should be made to avoid this type of problem in the future?Consider changes to policies and procedures, training, etc.

2. Lastly, consider "What did you learn from this problem solving?"Consider new knowledge, understanding and/or skills.

3. Consider writing a brief memo that highlights the success of the problemsolving effort, and what you learned as a result. Share it with your supervisor,peers and subordinates.

Step 12: Rational Versus Organic Approach to ProblemSolving

Rational person

A person with this preference often prefers using a comprehensive and logicalapproach similar to the guidelines in the above section. For example, the rationalapproach, described below, is often used when addressing large, complex mattersin strategic planning.

1.Define the problem.

2. Examine all potential causes for the problem.

3. Identify all alternatives to resolve the problem.

4. Carefully select an alternative.

5. Develop an orderly implementation plan to implement that best alternative.

6. Carefully monitor implementation of the plan.

7. Verify if the problem has been resolved or not.

A major advantage of this approach is that it gives a strong sense of orderin an otherwise chaotic situation and provides a common frame of reference fromwhich people can communicate in the situation. A major disadvantage of thisapproach is that it can take a long time to finish. Some people might argue,too, that the world is much too chaotic for the rational approach to be useful.

Organic person

Some people assert that the dynamics of organizations and people are not nearlyso mechanistic as to be improved by solving one problem after another. Often,the quality of an organization or life comes from how one handles being "onthe road" itself, rather than the "arriving at the destination." The quality comes from the ongoing process of trying, rather than from havingfixed a lot of problems. For many people it is an approach to organizationalconsulting. The following quote is often used when explaining the organic (orholistic) approach to problem solving.

A major advantage of the organic approach is that it is highly adaptable tounderstanding and explaining the chaotic changes that occur in projects andeveryday life. It also suits the nature of people who shun linear and mechanisticapproaches to projects. The major disadvantage is that the approach often providesno clear frame of reference around which people can communicate, feel comfortableand measure progress toward solutions to problems.

Examples of solution of Teaching Social Problem steps
The teaching social problem suitation

Kids and young adults need to be able to problem-solve on their own. Every day, kids are faced with a huge number of social situations and challenges. Whether they are just having a conversation with a peer, working with a group on a project, or dealing with an ethical dilemma, kids must use their social skills and knowledge to help them navigate tough situations. Ideally, we want kids to make positive choices entirely on their own. Of course, we know that kids don't start off that way. They need to learn how to collaborate, communicate, cooperate, negotiate, and self-advocate.

Social problem solving skills are critical skills to learn for kids with autism, ADHD, and other social challenges. Of course, all kids and young adults benefit from these skills. They fit perfectly into a morning meeting discussion or advisory periods for older kids. Not only are these skills that kids will use in your classroom, but throughout their entire lives. They are well worth the time to teach!

Here are 5 steps to help kids learn social problem solving skills:

Step 1:

Teach kids to communicate their feelings. Being able to openly and respectfully share emotions is a foundational element to social problem solving. Teaching I statements can be a simple and effective way to kids to share their feelings. With an I statement, kids will state, "I feel _______ when ______." The whole idea is that this type of statement allows someone to share how their feeling without targeting or blaming anyone else. Helping kids to communicate their emotions can solve many social problems from the start and encourages positive self-expression.

Step 2:

Discuss and model empathy. In order for kids to really grasp problem-solving, they need to learn how to think about the feelings of others. Literature is a great way teach and practice empathy! Talk about the feelings of characters within texts you are reading, really highlighting how they might feel in situations and why. Ask questions like, "How might they feel? Why do you think they felt that way? Would you feel the same in that situation? Why or why not?" to help teach emerging empathy skills. You can also make up your own situations and have kids share responses, too.

Developing Empathy

Step 3:

Model problem-solving skills. When a problem arises, discuss it and share some solutions how you might go forward to fix it. For example, you might say, "I was really expecting to give the class this math assignment today but

I just found out we have an assembly. This wasn't in my plans. I could try to give part of it now or I could hold off and give the assignment tomorrow instead. It's not perfect, but I think I'll wait that way we can go at the pace we need to." This type of think-aloud models the type of thinking that kids should be using when a problem comes up.

Step 4:

Use social scenarios to practice. Give a scenario and have kids consider how that person might feel in that situation. Discuss options for what that person might do to solve the problem, possible consequences for their choices, and what the best decision might be. Kids can consider themselves social detectives by using the clues and what they know about social rules to help them figure out the solution. These are especially fun in small groups to have kids discuss collaboratively. Use these free social problem solving cards to start your kids off practicing!

Social Problem Solving Task Cards

Step 5:

Allow kids to figure it out. Don't come to the rescue when a child or young adult has a problem. As long as it's not a serious issue, give them time to think about it and use their problem-solving skills on their own. Of course, it's much easier to have an adult solve all the problems but that doesn't teach the necessary skills. When a child comes to you asking for your help with a social problem, encourage them to think about it for five minutes before coming back to you. By that point, they might have already figured out possible solutions and ideas and might not even need you anymore. If you are interested in helping your kids learn social problem solving skills right away, consider trying out these Social Problem Solving Task Cards. They highlight real social scenarios and situations that kids can discuss. The scenarios include a variety of locations, such as in classrooms, with family, with friends, at recess, and at lunch. This set is targeted for elementary-age learners.

CHAPTER TWO

MANAGEMENT SCIENCE PROBLEMS SOLUTION CASES

Case 1

How reduces transport cost of shipping or road transportation to the most minimum level in warehouse, factory locations

linear programming management science solution method :

Researching the main shipping or /and road transport problem to bring cost rising to between either warehouse or/and factory or both and the goods transfer transport destinations.

Inventory Models management science method helps warehouse, factory locations to reduce road or shipping transporation cost between goods transfer locations. For certain types of inventory control problems, certain models that attempt to minimize the cost associated with ordering and carrying inventories have been developed.

Transportation problem is a particular class of linear programming, which is associated with day-to-day activities in our real life and mainly deals with logistics. It helps in solving problems on distribution and transportation of resources from one place to another. The goods are transported from a set of sources (e.g., factory) to a set of destinations (e.g., warehouse) to meet the specific requirements. In other words, transportation problems deal with the transportation of a single product manufactured at different plants (supply origins) to a number of different warehouses (demand destinations). The objective is to satisfy the demand at destinations from the supply constraints at the minimum transportation cost possible. To achieve this objective, we must know the quantity of available supplies and the quantities demanded. In addition, we must also know the location, to find the cost of transporting one unit of commodity from the place of origin to the destination. The model is useful for making strategic decisions involved in selecting optimum transportation routes so as to allocate the production of various plants to several warehouses or distribution centers. Suppose there are more than one centers, called 'origins' , from where the goods need to be transported to more than one places called 'destinations' and the costs of transporting or shipping from each of the origin to each of the destination being different and known. The problem is to transport the goods from various origins to different destinations in such a manner that the cost of shipping or transportation is minimum. Thus, the transportation problem is to transport various amounts of a single homogenous commodity, which are initially stored at various origins, to different destinations in such a way that the transportation cost is minimum.

Inventory Models Management Science Solution Method

A tyre manufacturing concern has many factories located in many different cities transport cost case

For certain types of inventory control problems, certain models that attempt to minimize the cost associated with ordering and carrying inventories have been developed. The objective of the transportation model is to determine the amount to be shipped from each source to each destination so as to maintain the supply and demand requirements at the lowest transportation cost.

For example: A tyre manufacturing concern has many factories located in many different cities. The total supply potential of manufactured product is absorbed by retail dealers in different cities of a country. Then, transportation problem is to determine the transportation schedule that minimizes the total cost of transporting tyres from various factory locations to various retail dealers.

The transportation model can also be used in making location decisions. The model helps in locating a new facility, a manufacturing plant or an office when two or more number of locations is under consideration. The total transportation cost, distribution cost or shipping cost and production costs are to be minimized by applying the model. How do you calculate the cheapest way to ship goods between several warehouses and stores? In this lesson, you will explore the transportation problem and its solutions.

Searching What Is The Transportation Problem to cholocate retail stores case

Mathematical Programming Management Science Solution Method:
It attempts to maximize the attainment level of one goal subject to a set of requirements and limitations. It has extensive use in business, economics, engineering, the military and public service, mainly as an aid to the solution of allocation problems.

Imagine yourself owning a small network of chocolate retail stores. To run a successful business, you will also have to own or rent a warehouse where you will store the goods ready to be delivered whenever the stores need them. If you have only one warehouse, it will be supplying all your stores. However, as soon as you expand and open a second warehouse, you will have to make an important decision: which warehouse will deliver which goods to each of your stores? Depending on the choice you make, you might save or spend a significant amount of money.

The transportation problem is a distribution-type problem, the main goal of which is to decide how to transfer goods from various sending locations (also known as origins) to various receiving locations (also known as destinations) with minimal costs or maximum profit. As long as the number of origins and destinations is low, this is a relatively easy decision. But as the numbers grow, this becomes a complicated linear programming problem. Think about Walmart. In 2016, it had 5,229 stores and 166 distribution centers in the US! It would be impossible to calculate the optimal shipping routes without a computer algorithm.

General transportion problem types
Transportation problems can be classified into different groups based on their main objective and origin supply versus destination demand. Transportation problems whose main objective is to minimize the cost of shipping goods are called minimizing. An alternative objective is to maximize the profit of shipping goods, in which case the problems are called maximizing.

In a case where the supply of goods available for shipping at the origins is equal to the demand for goods at the destinations, the transportation problem is called balanced. In a case where the quantities are different, the problem is unbalanced.

When a transportation problem is unbalanced, a dummy variable is used to even out demand and supply. A dummy variable is simply a fictional warehouse or store. For example, if total supply at all warehouses is 50 units, but total demand at all stores is only 40 units, we create a fictional store with an additional demand of 10 units. The cost of shipping to the fictional store is usually zero. Now, the transportation problem becomes balanced. It is worth noting that sometimes problems that are solved using the transportation method have nothing to do with an actual movement of goods. What is crucial for applying the method is to recognize the network of connected elements.

Case 2

Management science solves public transport passenger queue problem
Waiting Line (Queuing) Models: solution imbalanced taxi and passenger queue in urban public transportation service case
The Four Problems Of Urban Transportation (And The Four Solutions)
The fixed-route bus and the bicycle solve at least one urban problem better than new technologies urban transportation problem case. There are four main problems in urban transportation that require four separate solutions. Some urban transportation design recommendion argued that technology can solve some problems, but not the same problem that public transit solves."The city has four separate problems of urban transportation which have four separate kinds of solutions, and it is very important to not mistake the solution for one problem for the solution for a different problem."
The first solution :
Bus stop time real -time information technology and apps solution method
Friction arises between a transit system and its users when the users don't have the information they need when they need it. That problem has been largely solved, Walker said, by information technology and apps. "That has been a fantastic transformation. Some of you may not be old enough to remember what life was like without real-time information, when you just went right out into the snow and wondered when the bus was coming."

The second solution:

Innovation method
The innovation method solves the city has four separate problems of urban transportation may include: Emissions and Energy Efficiency: "for which we're currently working on electric vehicles, and that's fantastic." Labor and Safety: The cost of labor is the primary driver of operation costs for passenger transport, Walker said. "It is why your bus doesn't come more often, and it is also why Uber can't make money." Autonomous vehicles will

address that and the accident rate. "There is a problem with the efficient use of labor, and also a colossal problem of safety for which we are talking about autonomous vehicles, and that's fantastic." Space: "And there is a fourth problem which is the efficient use of space, for which the solution is on the one hand, cycling and walking, and on the other, public transit provided by big vehicles."

The third soution:

The fixed-route bus or train solutione method is the best solution reason
The fixed-route bus or train is the vehicle of the future, because it remains the most efficient way to move large numbers of people through the congested space of a city. In his critique of public transit, Musk pointed out that people prefer "individualized transport, that goes where you want, when you want," like the Tesla Model S. But Walker contends individualized transport that goes where you want when you want can't move people through a congested city as efficiently as a fixed-route bus.

"We are always going to need vehicles sized to the appropriate capacity requirement, which means big buses in big cities," he said. "Our friends in the tech industry, including many of you here, and I love what you're doing, are always trying to sell us stories about how everything will fit together into a magnificent fusion. They want us to mix it up, to think about how it combines. And I'm always saying, but wait a minute, if you're going to be a smart customer you have to think about how they work separately as well."

Instead of above technological methods to solve public transport problem. The queue control management method will be one good solution How do I conduct queue management of passengers in waiting taxi or bus area for Public transportation Vehicles?

Are there existing design projects and studies that a public transportation vehicle (Taxi or Bus) would know the number of passenger in waiting area/ shed through long range network? I am conducting a design project for buses in my country that would know the number of passenger in waiting area and this information will be sent to the terminal or bus which will they used to pick up these passengers. Thus, congestion of buses and passenger can be lessen

I think that there are 2 technical issues: a) how to collect and transmit information, b) how to manage public transportation to minimize queue. About the 1st question you probably need either to do it manually (operator sitting at every station and making phone calls like "please send one more bus urgently, we have 100 of people waiting here", but this may be too expensive, at least for city buses) or to do it automatically (video camera, some image recognizing software that calculates people and then sends a message to the center) in this city has four separate problems of urban transportation concerns taxi and bus queue case.

Conclusion of the best solution method

As I know, there is not such a system design yet. but you may devise one by using the queue theory and optimizing the performance of the system by the following pattern:

- defining a objective function corresponding to the total passengers awaiting time.

- optimizing the objective function by finding the best set of assigning the available buses to the stations (considering the routes)

Case 3

Waiting Line (Queuing) Models: solution imbalanced taxi and passenger queue in airport case

Predicting Imbalanced Taxi and Passenger Queue Contexts in Airport management problem

For certain types of problems involving queues, special descriptive models have been developed to predict the performance of service systems such as car garages – cars standing in queue for servicing.

The taxi and passenger queue contexts indicate the various states of queues related to taxis and passengers (i.e. taxis are waiting for passengers, passengers are waiting for taxis, both are waiting for each other, none is waiting). Predicting these queue contexts in a future time is very important for better airport ground transport operations. However, queue context prediction at the airport is a challenging problem due to the presence of different contextual factors i.e., time, weather, taxi trips, flight arrivals and many more. Also these taxi and passenger queue contexts at the airport are imbalanced since some of the contexts are very infrequently occurring compared to others. In this paper, we address the problem of predicting imbalanced taxi and passenger queue contexts at the airport. First, we investigate different contextual factors, including time, taxi trips, passengers and weather for queue context prediction. Then we propose a detailed step by step solution to address this problem. To support the effectiveness of our detailed approach, we generate a queue context dataset by fusing three real world datasets including taxi trip, passenger wait time and weather condition that represent the taxi and passenger queue contexts at any major international airport in any country City. The experimental results demonstrate that our developed queue context prediction framework provides detailed solutions to deliver higher accuracy in queue context prediction.

Therefore, context-aware mobility analytics enables the provision of intelligent analysis on mobility contexts considering different user perspectives. The success of many applications such as transport management and location recom- mendation requires the discovery of valuable knowledge through extensive analysis of related factors . For example, an airport can be regarded as the first and last impression of a city. Since a longer passenger wait time for a taxi ride can diminish the satisfaction rating of an airport , the authorities try hard to maintain a higher customer satisfaction rating by providing various mobility services such as easy and comfortable airport transfer to the city using taxicabs. However, the demand-supply equilibrium of taxis is highly dependent on the taxi drivers' decisions to make airport trips. The ubiquitous data can help with managing the mobility of airport users by detecting different mobility contexts (i.e. situa- tions of the concurrent queues related to passengers and taxis) . The intelligent analysis and prediction of different mobility contexts can help with making mobility decisions for airport passengers and taxis at different times of the day.

We argue that by incorporating the temporal deviation of taxi drivers' moves as the feature importance score can identify good quality neighborhoods and thus significantly boost the taxi-passenger queue context prediction accuracy. We utilize a real world queue context data set that includes information from taxi trip logs, airport passenger arrivals and weather conditions which are relevant to the different queue contexts. Then we propose a temporal driver-knowledge deviation based feature importance scheme to select a quality neighborhood for predicting taxi and passenger queue contexts.

As we extract more features by computing the deviations of all feature values from its hourly mean along with the current features of the queue context dataset , it is necessary to check the relevancy of all features. The reason is that the use of all these features may degrade the prediction performance significantly due to the inclusion of some irrelevant and redundant features. Also, for different stations, the configurations such as lane numbers, and maximum queue length of taxis and passengers can affect the solution of the passenger-taxi queue problem.

The proliferation of pervasive devices in smart cities has enabled the development of many smart mobility applications . Smart parking is one of the innovations that provides easy to use parking services to the urban commuters by leveraging pervasive sensors and flexible payment systems. Inferring a situational awareness map using clustering methods has become a popular research topic in recent years. GPS trajectory has been utilised in smart mobility applications. In this section, we briefly review the related work which can be separated into two categories: points clustering and trajectory clustering. For example, intelligent reminders of user activities and notifications for major transporta- tion delays due to the current situation of the users. This outcome can also be leveraged for the applications of discovering user rou- tines based on personal contexts of mobile users. In an intelligent healthcare scenario, a robust and simultaneous recogni- tion of multiple user contexts would be important to be considered for elderly and disabled people, while travelling through various accessible paths .

Case 4

Management games model solves salespeople emotion problem in store environment

Any organizations can let salespeople feel happy to sell their products. Then their sale performance will also raise. The question concerns that how to make them to feel happy to help the organization to sell their products? I shall explain how to apply managment games or management psychological methods to solve this organizational problem as below:

How to manage sales for predictable revenue?

In order to hold salespeople sale psychology whether they feel happy or unhappy, executives need to understand the essential activities, sales managers must focus on to be analysts for change, foster continuous improvement and create a sales culture that drives results. Sale executives need to know how to achieve top objectives of sales management is to drive sales, capture new revenue and exceed monthly sales and margin objectives, e.g. performing sale straregy development with each salesperson on Monday morning at a minimum, and in a formal one-on-one meeting during the week;using strategy tools and questioning techniques to ensure the prospects are qualified and the strategy is valid; knowing the ratio between future values and future monthly quotos to raise sale opportunities; six month on-going sale plan aims to make sure there are coordinated to achieve sale to various market segments; developing on ongoing series of networking events to build market awareness in order to ensure all salespeople attend specific events involved in networking by salespeople to, understanding the market how to influence salespeople sale method to sale number, understanding trends and seeking some channels to raise additional sales opportunities; how to create trained or warm sale environment to let sales teams feel happy to sell.

How to design and utilize efficient control sale procedures?

The sale cycle procedure may include these market activities, such as advertising, sales promotion, market research, physical distribution, pricing , sale place, sale staffs seeking. SO, any organizations need have good sale planning, direction and control of the personnel, selling activities of a business with including recruiting, selecting, training, rating, supervising, paying or reward system, motivating strategy , as all these tasks apply to the personnel sales-force.

The factors may influence salespeople psychology, they may include fair income reward system, or appreciation methods and sale career development plan to every salesperson. It aims to encourage them to achieve the highest sale effort. Anymore, methods to train sale managers have the right direction to guide, lead and motivate their salespeople, e.g. knowledge of salespeople psychology needs how to satisfy them, understanding why they choose to do or act themselves sale behaviors in order to improve their weakness to motivate salespeople to achieve company's sale target goal every month easily, e.g. raising profitability, sales volume, market share, growth and corporate image building raise clients' confidence to choose to buy this company's any products more easily.

The sales organization is required for the following purposes, they may include: enabling top-management, to devote to more time in policy making for the growth and expansion of business to divide and fix authority among the subordinates , so that they may shirk work, to avoid repetition of duties and functions, so that there may not be any confusion among them to locate responsibility of each and every employee , so that they can complete the whole work in stipulated time, if not then the particular person must be responsible, to establish the sales effort to enforce proper supervision of sales force.

What does the concept of salespeople replacement value mean?

What is a sales force turnover management tool?

Sales force turnover is defined as the rate at which salespeople leave an organizations, resignations, retirements or dismissals. So, if the organization can raise the sales force turnover ratio, because many salespeople can be promoted or the retirement, or the sales force turnover ratio raising reasons as well as they are not resignation or dismissal reasons. I believe that the organization ought have good sale environment and reasonable reward and welfare strategy to let its salespeople feel happy to help this company to sell its products every day.

However, sales management's actions have direct or indirect effects to impact on turnover. Direct effects may include the firm's firing or dismiss policy. The indirect effects on sale turnover may include new salesperon recruiting and selecting policies affect the quality and performance of the sale force as well as the speed at which salespeople are replaced. The same policies have an impact on the sales force turnover rate through the characteristics of the newly recurited salespersons and the promotion , training, retraining policies, support, supervision, compensation. ALl of those factors have an impact on salesperson's personal satisfaction or dissatisfaction absolutely. So, any sale organizations need to concern how and why whether any one of above these factors may influence their salespeople how to perform or act sale behaviors in order to excite their sale number more effective in long term.

How to achieve sale force management effectively?

Sale management is one strategy to many organizations, because organizations expect their salespeople can only raise product sale number. So , they will consider whetther how to implement the sale management strategy to be the most suitable to themselves sale organizations in order to excite their sale teams to sell their products to achieve sale growth aim effectively. So for organization's long term sale growth development, it seems that one excellent sale management strategy can help the organization has stable sale number growth in long term possible.

However, the term " selling" includes a variety of sales situations and activities. For example, those sales positions where the sales representative is required primarily to deliver the product to the customer on a regular or periodic basis. The emphasis is this type of sales activity is very different to the sales position where the sales representative is dealing with sales of capital equipment to industrial purchasers. IN additions some sales representatives deal only in export markets whereas others sell direct to customers in their homes. So, sale organizations need to sell to local or overseas market as well as its target customer is businessmen or individual consumer or both in order to implement to choose their most suitable sale management strategy to train their salespeople more effective or achieving sale growth objective only. Because these its sale major target and where sale market place both factors will influence how it ought train its salespeople, so any organization's training method ought be influenced to change by whom is its major sale target and where is its major sale market location factors.

How to know the psychology of salesmanship?

When the organization can predict or find reasons to explain why its salespeople feel unhappy to help

this organization to sell its products. Then, it can attempt to improve its weaknesses in order to let its salespeople to feel more sale service satisfactory feeling to continue to help this organization to sell its products. Then, it won't need not often to train or recruit new salespeople to replace its old salespeople in consequence.

How to know what its salespeoples' real need in order to raise their sale service satisfactory feeling ?

Psychology means that " science of the mind" and psychology plays to important part in business and it is quite worth to bring to influence any organization salespeoples' posivitive or negative sale emotion in their every sale process between themselves and their every client in personal. For example, if the salesperson often have negative emotion or he feels unhappy in every sale process, then he will encounter or increase many times of sale failure possibilities. He will feel that he is one poor verbal advertiser or seller or promotor to help his organization to promote its products to sell again as well as he will lose confidence to sell any products next sale chance, because his failure sale experiences are accumulated to influence his sale emotion to be poor or difficult sale.

Hence, the poor performance salesperson needs have more successful sale experiences to compensate his / her prior many sale failure times feeling, if the organization hopes this poor performance salesperson can raise sale number easily. Overall, any organizations need to concern how to improve or raise the more failure times of sale experience salespeoples' sale techniques or methods or attitudes more than choose to fire or dismiss them as well as finding another new salesperson to replace him/her. Because it is possible that the salesperson 's poor sale performance that is not due to himself/herself poor sale effort and sale knowledge or lacking sale experience to the product, it may be due to the poor sale team cooperation relationship , feeling poor or not comfortable sale physcial shop environment, poor sale manager and other salespeople working relationship, the sale manager lacks leadership effort, poor family relationship etc. external factors more than himself/herself personal poor or negative emotion or poor health etc. personal factors. Hence, the organization ought enquire him/her why he/she feels unhappy to sell its products and it needs to attempt to find methods to solve his/her challenges immediately. If his/her challenges can be solved. It is possible that his/her sale efforts can be also raised for. So, if the organization can know how to utilize positive sale emotion psychological methods to predict or know why and how every salesperson perform his/her sale behavior in whose daily sale tasks, then it can concentrate on implementing effective and the most suitable sale training to raise their sale abilities more easily.

However, the sale training may include: How to build or improve long term good salesperson and his/her customer sale service relationship between every salesperson and every client in every buying and selling cycle process, how to using right communicating styleds for better understanding every client's real needs, powers and negotiating, e.g. every salesperson needs to review why there are many clients do not choose to buy any products from his sale presentation or promotion, finding every time sale failure reasons can let the salesperson makes himself/herself sale failure reasons evaluation or judgement in order to find what is the major reason influences his/her sale failure, e.g. lacking product knowledge, he/she often let many clients to feel that he lacks patience to listen the client's enquiry or feedback, his sale presentation is not attractive to let many clients like to stay longer time to listen his sale presentation in whole sale process, the salesperson himself/herself emotion is negative and he /she can let many clients feel he / she is not happy or does not enjoy to sell this product from himself/herself face impression or sale behavior impression easily, lacking enough sale techniques to persuade his/her clients why he/she ought choose to buy this product in whole sale process etc. these factors may influence the salesperson's sale failure chance to be raised. Hence sales manager ought need to spend long time to meet the poor sale performance salesperson to discuess what his/her sale challenges are the most major to influence his/her every sale successful chance in order to improve his/ her sale performance more successfully.

In conclusion, the reasons why salespeople often encounter sale failure possibilities. The factors may include these aspects, such as they lask the desire to help customers to make satisfactory purchase decisons, they only concern how to achieve sale final objective or aim only, it will cause clients feel they do not real concern their real needs. They only concern to sell the product in success. They do not know how to describe the product whether what characteristics or features it owns accurately in order to increase sale chance to persudade them to make final decision to by the product, they do not attempt to participate the whole sale process to help them to choose the most right product in order to satisfy their any purcahse needs, they ought avoid deceptive or manipulative influence tactics, avoid the use of high pressure sales techniques etc. Thus, if any organizations can spend time to investigate what factors cause why any one of salespeople choose perform his/her sale behavior often in order to know or understand their salespeople' sale psychology absolutely. Then, I believe that their sale number will only grown more easily.

Case 5

Markov Chains Management Science Method : Persuading or exciting property buyers' property purchase choice in preference

Markov Chains Management Science Method means that it is used for predicting the outcome of processes where systems or units change their condition over time (e.g., consumers change their preferences for certain brands of commodities).

Something Behavioral (e.g., Prospect Theory) excites to property buyer preference choice to the property developer

What Is the Prospect Theory?

Prospect theory assumes that losses and gains are valued differently, and thus individuals make decisions based on perceived gains instead of perceived losses. Also known as the "loss-aversion" theory, the general concept is that if two choices are put before an individual, both equal, with one presented in terms of potential gains and the other in terms of possible losses, the former option will be chosen.

How the Prospect Theory Works ?

Prospect theory belongs to the behavioral economic subgroup, describing how individuals make a choice between probabilistic alternatives where risk is involved and the probability of different outcomes is unknown. This theory was formulated in 1979 and further developed in 1992 by Amos

Tversky and Daniel Kahneman, deeming it more psychologically accurate of how decisions are made when compared to the expected utility theory.

The underlying explanation for an individual's behavior, under prospect theory, is that because the choices are independent and singular, the probability of a gain or a loss is reasonably assumed as being 50/50 instead of the probability that is actually presented. Essentially, the probability of a gain is generally perceived as greater. Although there is no difference in the actual gains or losses of a certain product, the prospect theory says investors will choose the product that offers the most perceived gains.

Tversky and Kahneman proposed that losses cause a greater emotional impact on an individual than does an equivalent amount of gain, so given choices presented two ways—with both offering the same result—an individual will pick the option offering perceived gains. For example, assume that the end result is receiving $25. One option is being given the straight $25. The other option is gaining $50 and losing $25. The utility of the $25 is exactly the same in both options. However, individuals are most likely to choose to receive straight cash because a single gain is generally observed as more favorable than initially having more cash and then suffering a loss.

Types of Prospect Theory

According to Tversky and Kahneman, the certainty effect is exhibited when people prefer certain outcomes and underweight outcomes that are only probable. The certainty effect leads to individuals avoiding risk when there is a prospect of a sure gain. It also contributes to individuals seeking risk when one of their options is a sure loss.

The isolation effect occurs when people have presented two options with the same outcome, but different routes to the outcome. In this case, people are likely to cancel out similar information to lighten the cognitive load, and their conclusions will vary depending on how the options are framed.

•The prospect theory says that investors value gains and losses differently, placing more weight on perceived gains versus perceived losses.

•An investor presented with a choice, both equal, will choose the one presented in terms of potential gains.

•The prospect theory is part of behavioral economics, suggesting investors chose perceived gains because losses cause a greater emotional impact.

•The certainty effect says individuals prefer certain outcomes over probable ones, while the isolation effect says individuals cancel out similar information when making a decision.

Prospect Theory Example

Consider an investor is given a pitch for the same mutual fund by two separate financial advisors. One advisor presents the fund to the investor, highlighting that it has an average return of 12% over the past three years. The other advisor tells the investor that the fund has had above-average returns in the past 10 years, but in recent years it has been declining. Prospect theory assumes that though the investor was presented with the exact same mutual fund, he is likely to buy the fund from the first advisor, who expressed the fund's rate of return as an overall gain instead of the advisor presenting the fund as having high returns and losses.

How and why behavioral economic method can predict house buyers house purchase need or desire whether the country's house buyers their house purchase need or desire will increase or decrease in the year. I shall explain the reasons as below:

Supply-side economists say that increasing business growth, not consumer demand, will boost the economy. They agree the government has a role to play, but fiscal policy should target companies. They rely on tax cuts and deregulation. So, supply-side economists believe that raising house buyers' house purchase or long term renting or instalement payment desires. Government or business organizations will play a important role, e.g. decresing salary tax, banks can charge low interest to encourage many people to borrow much long term loan or money to spend long term expenditure, e.g. buying house. So, it seems that other parties will encourage house buyers' house purchase more more than themselves psychological feeling influence. Otherwise, demand-side economists say that any house buyer individual psychological living need desire is more influential to encourage they choose to buy house in preference. On one hand, in demand-side economists view, I shall apply behavioral economic concept to explain why and how causes house buyer individual house purchase choice in preference than rent choice . On the other hand, in supply-side economists view, I shall apply demand and supply economic concept to explain why and how casues house buyer individual house purchase choice in preference than rent choice in property market.

What does behavioral economy mean ?Think about supposing you plan to buy a house. You may have decided to simplify your decision making by opting for the house price, living environment, such as air and noise pollution, income level, school, public library, public park, public swimming pool, transportation facilities etc. different factors to influence you house purchase decision in the location. You may then have visited the house location to view its environments before you decide to choose the location to buy the house to live. But the decision making process did not stop there, as you now had to customize your model by visiting from different house location . You aim to compare whether anywhere location(s) can let you to feel the location is better to let you feel to live.) Instead the house location and environment factor, you were still considered the house appearance and design and comfortable feeling features you really needed. At this stage, most property developers will show a base model with options that can be changed according to whether the house buyers their preferences are environment, house design, house price, facilties before they decide to buy the house to live. The way in which these different location of house choices are presented to house buyers will influence the final house purchases made and illustrates a number of concepts from behavioral economic (BE) theories.

First, the base model shown in the customization engine represents a rational choice to any house buyers' purchase decision usually. Usually, house buyers, they will visit the house location to feel its living environment, entertainment facilities supply, transport facilities supply and house design and comfortable feeling to decide to buy the house to live, instead of income factor in house market. The more uncertain house customers are about their rational house feeling , such as comfortable living, environment and facility and house design decision, instead of income factor influences can change their earlier first house purchase decision if they feel the house price is more expensive to compare the other houses choices.

Second, the house developer can frame options differently by employing either an 'add' or 'delete' customization mode (or something in between). In an add mode, house buyers start with a base model and then add more or better options. In a delete frame, the opposite process occurs, whereby house buyers have to deselect options or downgrade from a fully-loaded model. Such as this house market case, past research suggests that house buyers end up choosing a greater number of features when they are in a delete rather than an add frame (Biswas, 2009). Finally, the option framing strategy will be associated with different house price anchors prior to customization, which may influence the perceived value of the house. If the final house ends up with one million house price bid, its cost is likely to be perceived as more attractive if the initial default configuration was two million house price (fully loaded) rather than one million house price. Why does the more expensive house price will still attract some house buyers to choose to buy in preference—an option framing strategy that maximizes sales, but set at a default house price that deters a minimum of potential house buyers from considering a purchase in the first place. When the house buyers group is high and stable income group, they won't consider the more expensive house price issue to influence them to change to buy the one million house price houses to live easily. Instead of after they view the house location to let them to feel that there have less transport facilities, e.g. bus, taxi, underground train, tram etc. public service transport tools are close to their living location, or tehy feel the natural environment is polluted to let they feel the can not breathe fresh air , or there are many factories are close to their houses to cause they feel dirty air, or traffic jam is serious to cause air pollution and noise pollution , or they feel that the two million house design is poor, they can not let them to feel comfortable to live in the appartments, it means that the house price is under value to be accepted to same to two million price. Then, the stable and high income house buyers will change their earlier house purchase first choice to accept the other house opitions to decide to buy in preference.

● Rational Expectations And Rational Theories excite or raise property market buyers ' perference property choice desires to the property developer method

●

What are Rational Expectations?

Rational expectations is an economic theory that states that individuals make decisions based on the best available information in the market and learn from past trends. Rational expectations suggest that people will be wrong sometimes, but that, on average, they will be correct.

Understanding the Concept of Rational Expectations

The idea of rational expectations was first developed by American economist John F. Muth in 1961. However, it was popularized by economists Robert Lucas and T. Sargent in the 1970s and was widely used in microeconomics as part of the new classical revolution.

The theory states the following assumptions:

•With rational expectations, people always learn from past mistakes.

•Forecasts are unbiased, and people use all the available information and economic theories to make decisions.

•People understand how the economy works and how government policies alter macroeconomic variables such as price level, level of unemployment, and aggregate output.

The rational expectations theory comes in weak and strong versions. The "strong" version assumes that actors are able to access all available information and make rational decisions based on the information.

The "weak" versions assume that people lack the time to access all relevant information but make decisions based on their limited knowledge. For example, if they buy cornflakes, it is "rational" to keep buying the same brand and not worry about getting perfect information about relative prices of other cornflakes brands.

Most macroeconomists today use rational expectations as an assumption in their analysis of policies. When thinking about the effects of economic policy, the assumption is that people will do their best to work out the implications.

The rational expectations approach is often used to test the accuracy of inflation forecasts. For example, Pet is an individual's forecast in year t-1 of the price level in year t. The actual price level is denoted by Pt. The difference between the actual price level and individual's forecast is the forecast error for year t. Pt − Pet = rt is the individual's forecast error in year t. With rational expectations, the forecast errors are due to unpredictable numbers. However, if people systematically under-predict or over-predict numbers, the price level expectations are not rational.

Under rational expectations, what happens today depends on the expectations of what will happen in the future. But what happens in the future also depends on what happens today. Many macroeconomic principles today are created with the assumption of rational expectations. The theory is also used by many new Keynesian economists because it fits well with their assumption that people want to pursue their own self-interest. If people's expectations were not rational, the economic decisions of individuals would not be as good as they are.

Adaptive Expectations

While individuals who use rational decision-making use the best available information in the market to make decisions, adaptive decision makers use past trends and events to predict future outcomes. This is also known as backward thinking decision-making.

Adaptive expectations can be used to predict inflation. If inflation increased in the previous year, people expect an increased rate of inflation in the following year. The formula for adaptive expectations is Pet = Pt -1. It shows that people expect the trend of inflation to be the same as last year.

People will change their expectations of any variable if there is a difference between what they were expecting and what actually occurred. However, if their expectations turned out to be right, their future expectations likely will not change.

Limitations of Adaptive Expectations

While adaptive expectations allow us to measure expected variables and actual variables, they are not as commonly used in macroeconomics as rational expectations because of their limitations. The adaptive model is simplistic because it assumes that people base their decisions based on past data. However, in the real world, past data is just one of the factors that influence future behavior. Rational expectations incorporate many factors into the decision-making process.

What is house buyer individual Rational Choice ?

In an ideal house market world, defaults, frames, and house price anchors would not have any bearing on consumer choices. House purchaser decisions would be the result of a careful weighing of costs and benefits and informed by existing preferences, such as whether the house future price will appreciate to raise value or reduce under value, the house living location will increase public transport facilities, public entertainment facilities, build more schools, offices to close to the house location. We would always make optimal decisions. In the 1976 book The Economic Approach to Human Behavior, the economist Gary S. Becker famously outlined a number of ideas known as the pillars of so-called 'rational choice' theory. The theory assumes that human actors have stable preferences and engage in maximizing behavior.

Mental Accounting management science method

The economist Richard Thaler, a keen observer of human behavior and founder of behavioral economics, was inspired by Kahneman & Tversky's work (see Thaler, 2015, for a summary). Thaler coined the concept of mental accounting. According to Thaler, people think of value in relative rather than absolute terms. They derive pleasure not just from an object's value, but also the quality of the deal – its transaction utility (Thaler, 1985). In addition, humans often fail to fully consider opportunity costs (tradeoffs) and are susceptible to the sunk cost fallacy. Why are people willing to spend more when they pay with a credit card than cash (Prelec & Simester, 2001)? Why would more individuals spend $10 on a theater ticket if they had just lost a $10 bill than if they had to replace a lost ticket worth $10 (Kahneman & Tversky, 1984)? Why are people more likely to spend a small inheritance and invest a large one (Thaler, 1985)? Such as this property market case, if the house living needer , he/she does not choose to pay all money to buy the house, although he/she has enough money to buy the house. He/she chooses to pay instalement or rent the house to live. If he/she own visa card. Then, he/she will choose to use visa card to pay rent or pay month instalement to the property developer's house in order to earn accumulated money reward or any benefits after he/she use the visa to pay the house rent or instalement every month. So, the visa card can encourage the house buyer to achieve the house rent or instalement payment house purchase long term transaction easily.

According to the theory of mental accounting, people treat money differently, depending on factors such as the money's origin and intended use, rather than thinking of it in terms of the "bottom line" as in formal accounting (Thaler, 1999). An important term underlying the theory is fungibility, the fact that all money is interchangable and has no labels. In mental accounting, people treat assets as less fungible than they really are. Even seasoned investors are susceptible to this bias when they view recent gains as disposable "house money" (Thaler & Johnson, 1990) that can be used in high-risk investments. In doing so, they make decisions on each mental account separately, losing out the big picture of the portfolio.

Another concept related to mental accounting captures the fact that people don't like to spend money. We experience pain of paying (Zellermayer, 1996), because we are loss averse. The pain of paying plays an important role in consumer self-regulation to keep spending in check (Prelec & Loewenstein, 1998). This pain is thought to be reduced in credit card purchases, because plastic is less tangible than cash, the depletion of resources (money) is less visible and payment is deferred. Different types of people experience different levels of pain of paying, which can affect spending decisions. Tightwads, for instance, experience more of this pain than spendthrifts. As a result, tightwads are particularly sensitive to marketing contexts that make spending less painful (Rick, 2018). Hence, such as this property market purchase case, because some house buyers do not hope to spend much money to buy one house to live. They will feel to use visa card, it can replace money to let them to feel they won't lose much money to spend in the moment. So, in mental spending feeling view, they will feel visa card will help them to reduce to spend much money to rent or pay instalement to live the house in long time. So, in psychological view, visa card is one good spending money replace tool to influence these non- accepted spend money buyers to make final house rent or paying instalement decision to live the house decision more easily.

Choice Overload managment science method

Humans' bounded rationality is particularly well illustrated by the concept of choice overload. Also referred to as 'overchoice', this phenomenon occurs as a result of too many choices being available to consumers. Overchoice has been associated with unhappiness (Schwartz, 2004), decision fatigue, going with the default option, as well as choice deferral—avoiding making a decision altogether, such as not buying a product (Iyengar & Lepper, 2000). Many different factors may contribute to perceived choice overload, including the number of options and attributes, time constraints, decision accountability, alignability and complementarity of options, consumers' preference uncertainty, among other factors (Chernev et al., 2015). Choice overload can be counteracted by simplifying choice attributes or the number of available options (Johnson et al., 2012). Hence, such as this property market case, when the month has too many properties are supplied to let house buyers to choose in the country's property market. Then, it will bring properties choice overload effect to cause the increasing houses number of options to cause the country's house buyers feel need to spend long time to make the house purchase preference decision in order to avoid any loss after they bought the under value houses to live. So, Choice overload usually cause long time choice process to any consumers, such as this property market consumption case.

Limited Information: The Importance of Feedback management science method

Bounded rationality's principle of limited knowledge or information is one of the topics discussed in the 2008 book Nudge. In the book, Thaler and Sunstein point to experience, good information, and prompt feedback as key factors that enable people to make good decisions. Consider climate change, for example, which has been cited as a particularly challenging problem in relation to experience and feedback. Climate change is invisible, diffuse, and a long-term process. Pro-environmental behavior by an individual, such as reducing carbon emissions, does not lead to a noticeable change. The same is true in the domain of health. Feedback in this area is often poor, and we are more likely to get feedback on previously chosen options than rejected ones.

Information Avoidance

Behavioral economics assumes that people are boundedly rational actors with a limited ability to process information. While a great deal of research has been devoted to exploring how available information affects the quality and outcomes of decisions, a newer strand of research has also explored situations where people avoid information altogether.

Information avoidance in behavioral economics (Golman et al., 2017) refers to situations in which people choose not to obtain knowledge that is freely available. Active information avoidance includes physical avoidance, inattention, the biased interpretation of information (see also confirmation bias) and even some forms of forgetting. In behavioral finance, for example, research has shown that investors are less likely to check their portfolio online when the stock market is down than when it is up, which has been termed the ostrich effect (Karlsson et al., 2009). More serious cases of avoidance happen when people fail to return to clinics to get medical test results, for instance (Sullivan et al., 2004).

While information avoidance is sometimes strategic, it can have immediate hedonic benefits for people if it prevents the negative (usually psychological) consequences of knowing the information. It usually carries negative utility in the long term, because it deprives people of potentially useful information for decision making and feedback for future behavior. Furthermore, information avoidance can contribute to a polarization of political opinions and media bias.

The impact of smoking, for example, is at best noticeable over the course of years, while its effect on cells and internal organs is usually not evident to the individual. Traditionally, generic feedback aimed at inducing behavioral change has been limited to information ranging from the economic costs of the unhealthy behavior to its potential health consequences (Diclemente et al., 2001). More recent behavior change programs, such as those employing smartphone apps to stop smoking, now usually provide positive and personalized behavioral feedback, which may include the number of cigarettes not smoked and money saved, along with information about health improvement and disease avoidance.

Predictably Irrational and Nudge alerted the public to a new breed of economists influenced by the study of behavioral decision making that was pioneered by Kahneman and Tversky's work (sometimes referred to as 'choice under uncertainty'). The psychology of homo economicus—a rational and selfish individual with relatively stable preferences—has been challenged, and the traditional view that behavior change should be achieved by informing, convincing, incentivizing or penalizing people has been questioned (Thaler & Sunstein, 2008). The field associated with this stream of research and theory is behavioral economics (BE), which suggests that human decisions are strongly influenced by context, including the way in which choices are presented to us. Behavior varies across time and space, and it is subject to cognitive biases, emotions, and social influences. Decisions are the result of less deliberative, linear, and controlled processes than we would like to believe.

Hence, such as this property market case, if the property developer can not provide more property advertisement to the property buyers to receive to let them to feel whether what benefits or enjoyment benefits that they can enjoy after they lived the property developer's houses to live. Due to lacking clear property information message to let many property buyers to know the property developer's property sale advertisement from property magazines, newspapers, TV, wesbite etc. channel. Then, it will influence the property developer's houses , they won't be many property buyers' choices, before they make final property purchase decision at the moment. So, property market purchase need desire change will be influenced by the time and space external unpredictable factor , such as visa card promotion , unemployment ratio rises up or falls down, the property advertisement attractive effort etc. unpredictable factors to excite any property buyers' living need desire in any time indirectly.

Dual-System Theory applies to property buyer market

Daniel Kahneman uses a dual-system theoretical framework (which established a foothold in cognitive and social psychology of the 1990s) to explain why our judgments and decisions often do not conform to formal notions of rationality. System 1 consists of thinking processes that are intuitive, automatic, experience-based, and relatively unconscious. System 2 is more reflective, controlled, deliberative, and analytical. Judgments influenced by System 1 are rooted in impressions arising from mental content that is easily accessible. System 2, on the other hand, monitors or provides a check on mental operations and overt behavior—often unsuccessfully.

Example 1: Availability and Affect

System 1 is 'home' of the heuristics (cognitive shortcuts) we apply and responsible for the biases (systematic errors) we may be left with when we make decisions (Kahneman, 2011). System 1 processes influence us when prior exposure to a number affects subsequent judgments, as evident in the anchoring effects discussed previously (Tversky & Kahneman, 1974). One of the most universal heuristics is the availability heuristic. Availability serves as a mental shortcut if the possibility of an event occurring is perceived as higher simply because an example comes to mind easily (Tversky & Kahneman, 1974); for instance, a person may deem pension investments too risky as a result of remembering a family member who lost most of her retirement savings in the recent recession. Readily available information in memory is also used when we make similarity-based judgments, as evident in the representativeness heuristic.

Finally, another 'general purpose' heuristic is that of affect, namely good or bad feelings that surface automatically when we think about an object. Applying the affect heuristic can lead to black-and-white thinking, which is particularly evident when people think about an object under conditions that hamper System 2 reflection, such as time pressure. For example, consumers may consider food preservatives' benefits as low and costs as high, thus leading to a significant negative risk-benefit correlation (Finucane, Alhakami, Slovic, & Johnson, 2000).

The role of affect in risky or uncertain situations is also evident in the risk-as-feelings model (Loewenstein, Weber, Hsee, & Welch, 2001). 'Consequentialist' accounts of decision making tend to focus on expectations along with the likelihood and desirability of possible outcomes. The risk-as-feelings perspective explains behavior in situations where emotional reactions to risk differ from cognitive evaluations. In these situations, behavior tends to be influenced by anticipatory feelings, emotions experienced in the moment of decision making.

Example 2: Salience

Availability and affect are processes internal to the individual that may lead to bias. The external equivalent of these processes is salience, whereby information that stands out, is novel, or seems relevant is more likely to affect our thinking and actions (Dolan et al., 2010). For example, a technological device can be framed as being 99% reliable or having only a 1% failure rate, thereby emphasizing either positive or negative information. Salience also underlies heuristic judgments that rely on external cues. Some psychologists have derived effort-reducing heuristics that simplify consumer decision making. The brand name heuristic, for example, suggests that salient cues in the form of brand names can be used to infer quality (Maheswaran, Mackie, & Chaiken, 1992). In terms of degrees of visual salience, one study found a congruence effect between price and font size, where showing a lower sale price in a small print size relative to the regular price resulted in greater purchase likelihood than presenting the sale price in a relatively large font (Coulter & Coulter, 2005). Finally, the salience of options can also be manipulated by rearranging the physical environment; for instance, a change as simple as moving water bottles closer to the cashier in a cafeteria has been shown to increase the salience and convenience of this healthier drink choice and thereby significantly boost water sales (Thorndike, Sonnenberg, Riis, Barraclough, & Levy, 2012).

Hence, such as this property market case, if the propety buyer feels that the property developer's house price won't be influenced to decrease easily in long time , even there are many property buyers still choose to buy the property developer's houses to live as well as the property developer's houses number supply won't increase in the long time. So, in Dual-System Theory explains if the house buyer felt that the property developer's house number supply won't increase, even decrease after there are many property buyers still chooce to buy its properties to live in preference in the country's property market. Then, the property developer's house high price and limited house supply factors will not influence the house buyer's prefer house choice decision more easily.

Property market demand and supply view

How can demand and supply determine property market price ? Property price is arrived at by the interaction between house buyers demand and property developers' houses number supply. Property price is dependent upon the house design and environment and facilities characteristics of both these fundamental components of a property market. Any properties demand and supply represent the willingness of house consumers and property developers to engage in properties buyers buying needs or desires. An exchange of a house purchasetakes place when properties buyers and properties sellers can agree upon a agreed property price. This module will look at property price in a competitive market. When imperfect property market competition exists such as with a property developer monopoly or single peoperty selling firm, property price outcomes may not follow the same general rules.

Equilibrium Price in property market

When a property exchange occurs, the agreed upon price is called an "equilibrium" property price, or a "market clearing" price. This equilibrium property price occurs at the intersection of house demand and house supply as presented are in balance at the moment in property market short time, e.g. one month.

Property price determination depends equally on the moment house buyers' living demand and the moment house number supply. It is truly a balance of the two market components. To see why the balance must occur, examine what happens when there is no balance, for example when the moment property market price is below than the past property market price, the property quantity demanded is greater than the property quantity supplied. In such a situation, property consumers would be clamouring for a property that property developers would not be willing to supply; a property shortage would exist. In this event, property consumers would choose to pay a higher price in order to get the property they want, while property developers would be encouraged by a higher price to bring more of the properties onto the property market.

The end result is a rise in property price, when the moment has many proprety buyers feel living desire needs. where the property supply and demand are in balance. Similarly, if a property price is above were chosen arbitrarily the property market would be in shortage properties are supplied, too less properties supply are relative to high living desire demand. If that were to happen, properties developers would be willing to take a higher price in order to sell, and property consumers would be induced by higher prices to increase their property purchases desire , because they feel afraid that there will have less properties to be supplied to sell later and their prices will continue to raise in long time.

Hence, a property market price is not necessarily a fair price, it is merely an outcome. It does not guarantee total living satisfaction on the part of house buyer and property seller. Typically some assumptions about the behaviour of property buyers and property sellers are made, which add a sense of reason to a property market price. For example, property buyers are expected to be self-living comfortable interested and, although they may not have perfect property living and house price knowledge, at least they will try to look out for their own living interests. Meanwhile, property sellers are considered to be profit maximizers. This assumption limits their willingness to sell to within a price range , high to low, where they can stay in business.

Change in Equilibrium Price of property market
When either property demand or supply shifts, the property equilibrium price will change. Look at the modules on understanding property number supply for a discussion of why of that property market component may move. So, what factors can influence the property equilibrium price to be raise.

Example 1: Unusually environment and facility factor
When the property's location , it's environment and facilities are improved to let property buyers feel to compare before. With no immediate change in property consumers' willingness to buy the property developer's houses to live in the location at the moment because they feel that its environment and facilities can not let them to feel enough and comfortable to live in the location, there is a movement along the reducing demand curve to a new low equilibrium market price. Property consumers will buy more but only at a lower house price, becaue they feel poor environment and not enough facilities supply to influence they do not choose the property developer's houses location in preference. Otherwise, if the property demand curve in this example were more vertical (more inelastic, it means that the property developers raise their price won't influence less property buyers because their living desire is increasing), the property price-quantity adjustments needed to bring about a new equilibrium between property demand and the new property supply would be different. Then compare the size of property price-property quantity changes in this with the first situation. With the same shift in property supply, equilibrium change in property price is larger when property demand is inelastic than when property demand is more elastic. The opposite is true for property quantity. A larger change in property quantity supply will occur when property demand is elastic compared with the property quantity change required when property demand is inelastic.

How Does Property Developer Supply and House Buyer Demand Affect the Housing Market?
Real estate is a tangible asset made up of property and the land on which it sits. Like other assets, real estate is also subject to supply and demand. The prices of homes, like stocks and bonds, depend heavily on the law of supply and demand. But just what kind of relationship does the housing market

have to this law? I suppose house supply number and house demad number , they must have close relationship to influence their house price changes in any time. Although, houses are expensive and fixed tangible asset, but they are still similar to general cheap product price changes to be influenced by demand and supply as below:

•The housing market relies very heavily on supply and demand.

•Housing demand and low supplies normally cause prices to rise.

•Prices drop when there is low demand and a larger supply of homes on the market.

•Low interest rates generally impact demand, while natural disasters, changing lifestyles, and the lack of available lots affect supplies.

The law of supply and demand is a basic economic principle that explains the relationship between supply and demand for a good or service, and how their interaction affects the price of that good or service. When there is high demand for a good or service, its price rises. If there is a large supply of a good or service but not enough demand for it, the price falls. The theory of supply and demand is one of the most basic principles in economics. Supply and demand work against each other until the point at which the equilibrium price is achieved—that is the price where supply is equal to demand in the market, such as property market case.

The law of demand dictates that people will have low or no demand for a good that has a higher price. That happens, of course, when all other factors remain equal. People tend to sacrifice something that comes at a higher cost, which curbs demand. Similarly, lower prices drive demand, meaning consumers value and purchase something more when it's cheaper. In fact, general property buyers' preference house purchase decision will be influenced by price factor in earlier. It is such as general cheap product demand and supply factor to influence its house price changes in any time. When it comes to the law of supply, prices drop when there is an increase in the supply of a good or service in the market. But when prices increase, the number of goods and services tend to drop. That's because it tends to cost more to produce and sell goods at a higher price.

Real Estate Supply and Demand economic theory

The housing market relies very heavily on supply and demand, which is why it is very prominent in the industry. Each housing transaction involves a buyer and a seller. The buyer places an offer on a property, leaving the seller to accept or reject the offer. The law of supply and demand dictates the equilibrium price of a property. Hence, supply and demand work against one another until the point at which a property's equilibrium price is reached.

A low property supply may drive prices up, which is what tends to happen with bidding wars. A specific property may be in demand by multiple parties who try to outbid each other by increasing their purchase price offer. The bidding war ends—depleting the supply—when the seller accepts one of the offers. When there is high demand for properties in a particular city or state, and a lack of supply of quality properties, the prices of houses tend to rise. When a weak economy and an oversupply of properties leads to low or no demand for housing, the prices of houses tend to fall.

Factors Affecting Housing Supply and Demand

Supply and demand is never an easy thing to measure in the real estate market. That's partly due because it takes a long time to construct new homes and fix up old ones to put back onto the market. Similarly, real estate is not like other industries in that it takes a lot of time to buy and sell homes and other properties. Some of the factors that influence housing demand include lower interest rates or borrowing costs in economic environment view. When interest rates are low, people are generally willing to take on more debt. They may be able to finance the purchase of a home because the amount of interest they have to pay isn't burdensome. If more buyers flood the market, demand for housing increases. And if there's a limited supply of housing inventory, that makes people in a low interest rate environment want to purchase even more.

Meanwhile, the supply of housing is in a constant state of change. Inventory may increase when people are moving—some may downsize, others may be try to make more room for an expanding family, while others may purchase their first home. Similarly, there may be an increase in development and new home construction, adding to the existing inventory. On the other hand, housing inventory decreases during times of natural disaster—such as floods and earthquakes—and when existing properties are demolished. Land is also a finite resource, so the amount of new developments is generally limited. It is unpredicted environmental factor to influence property price changes in the moment.

Economic environment factor influences property price changes

One of the major causes of the Great Recession that followed the financial crisis in the mid-2000s was the housing market crash. It was a direct result of the law of supply and demand. During the lead up to the financial crisis, consumers were enjoying relatively low borrowing rates. Banks began to offer low rates on mortgages, and were encouraged to relax their lending standards. People who weren't otherwise able to afford a home now found themselves able to realize their dreams. These consumers, called subprime borrowers, were able to snag a home with low down payments and low credit scores.

During this time, speculative buyers also began entering the market, driving up demand for housing and, at the same time, cutting in to the available supply. All of this, in turn, drove prices up to very lofty levels. The market couldn't keep up, and investors who were merely in the market to make some money—many were buying and flipping homes in a very short period of time—began pulling out of the market. Demand started to drop and, so did prices. The collapse of the real estate market in 2007 created an oversupply of houses and decreasing properties prices. Real estate prices depend on the law of supply and demand. When the demand for property is high but property is scarce, prices skyrocket and it becomes a seller's market. When the number of available properties increases to glut the market, prices typically drop. Supply and demand in real estate aren't easy to balance. Creating more saleable properties takes time, considerable work, and a lot of effort. It's not possible at all in some cases, and even when it is, it might not be possible for supply to increase in time to meet consumer demand. So, salespeoples' house sale experiences can also influence the property developer's house sale number.

Understanding this basic economic principle can help consumers decide the best time to buy or sell their properties.

Property market Over-Supply Or Under-Supply factor
You can usually expect a drop in prices when there is an over-supply of homes or land in a given area. You can't move the overage to another area to keep prices stable. Scarcity causes prices to rise when there isn't enough land or if there aren't enough homes in a given area. Even if land is available on which to build more homes, the time it takes to construct them cannot meet immediate property needs, so demand will remain constant or rise. Many forces that might have little or no impact on other regions influence local markets and vice versa. Pay attention to the factors that influence your local market. Watch local businesses and make note of upsizing and downsizing trends if you do business in a market that has jobs and many

workers relocating there. You'll also want to keep an eye on these issues if you're a homeowner looking to sell in such an area or if you're looking for property to purchase.

Things like divorce rates, death rates, and demographics can factor in. Factors that can greatly impact property market supply and demand—and by extension your business—might include local weather trends, an aging population, and investment trends if you do business in a resort area that includes vacation homes. Trends that impact discretionary income have more of an influence on this type of market than others. Trends in interest rates, national home prices, new housing starts, and many other economic indicators can influence real estate markets as well. These national events might not typically move real estate supply and demand directly, but they can render it less or more important. The mood and sentiments of the buying public cannot be overlooked. Supply and demand don't exist in a vacuum. But few could afford to pay those prices in a worsening economy and even those who could were understandably reluctant to part with their money at that time. So properties sat on the market, unsold. Worried homeowners in financial distress put their homes up for sale rather than risk foreclosure. Remember, almost 9 million jobs were lost during the Great Recession. Now what happens? Supply begins surpassing demand by leaps and bounds. The housing market is glutted and those healthy prices evaporate—which has little to do with local factors except as they're an extension of national woes.

Land Parcels Are Finite factor to influence property market price

If the country has high population, but land supply is less to let property developers to find lands to build houses easily. Such as Hong Kong is one high population and small city. So, its property prices must be higher to compare other countries, and it causes that its rooms and houses size or area is small , but house sale price or rent is still high.

Such as Hong Kong house market case, Hong Kong people cannot fill a real estate supply shortage by manufacturing more units of land. It's a finite supply, not a manufactured commodity. Hong Kong people might be able to create more units within a given space, such as condos or townhouses, but the land itself is unique and cannot be duplicated to accommodate a short supply. When a shortage of land for homes exists in a given area, Hong Kong people can't simply move in more land to alleviate the shortage. Real estate is where it sits. It will always be a local commodity influenced by local conditions. In short, keep up with the big picture but narrow your primary focus to your region. Supply and demand in real estate will always be foremost a local issue.

As with many other types of business market, the property market is driven by supply and demand. Property prices fluctuate depending upon the factors that influence both supply and demand. Knowledge of these factors equips you with the capability of knowing when to rent/buy and, perhaps just as importantly, when to sell. At the most basic level, when property supply is greater than demand, prices fall. That's the nature of almost every product. Similarly, when the demand for properties is greater than the available supply, prices rise. Even though property markets have these principles in common with many other types of products or business services, there are some differences worth mentioning. For example, the real estate market also takes into consideration factors such as location, seasonality, and durability. There are also different types of real estate – residential, industrial, commercial and land – each of which has their own factors that influence market supply and demand. "Real estate" is defined as more than just property. It also includes natural resources and land, too. So, Hong Kong property market's price is influenced by land supply factor more than other factors, such as facilities , environment , transport etc. factors influence.

Local factors that influence property rates include:

1 – Restrictions on property production – for instance, in the case of Manhatten, there is not much space for added supply. As a result, demand remains high and prices even higher.

2 – Credit access – this often depends on where individuals live. Rural communities may have less access to bank credit, for example – reducing demand.

3 – Job market – the more jobs, the greater the demand for properties.

4 – Transport – better transport translates into greater desirability for people to move – increasing demand.

5 – Retired persons – retired people often decide to downsize and opt for a smaller property in a different locality, thereby increasing supply.

6 – Families – as families begin to grow, they need greater sized properties. This increases the demand for larger homes, whilst decreasing demand for smaller homes.

7 – Meteorology – destinations with more favorable weather profiles and ones that avert the extremes of weather are preferable. Demand in places

such as San Diego is significantly higher than the tornado alleys of Alabama.

8 – Income – if income levels in a locality are generally high, there is more money in the market to purchase homes, decreasing supply and increasing prices.

9 – Construction market – the greater the degree of construction of new properties, the greater the supply in the market.

Understanding the factors that drive market supply and demand, and hence property prices are important. The more informed about these nine factors, the better purchasing/selling decisions you can make. For example – designs and styles and fads come and go into "fashion", and what design/style/fad factors elevate a property price one-year can diminish the price of a property the following year. If you are managing a property, you can factor these decisions when determining optimum rent or a selling value.

When borrowing rates are lower, properties become more affordable. This, too, influences demand. Tax credits, for example – for first-time buyers – can encourage more buyers to seek interest in the property market. As well as this, there are various social factors involved, too – such as the social status afforded to people who own their own homes. Age can come into play here, too, depending on the city and what social expectations young professionals have.

What drives property market supply and demand, then, is an interweaving network of factors, many of which playoff on one another. It's important to appreciate the impact that each of these individual factors has and how they influence property prices throughout the country.

How to Analyze Supply and Demand For Apartment Buildings

One of the most important ways to use all of the data gathered in a real estate market analysis is to examine the supply and demand factors for a particular type of real estate. For example, an investor considering the construction or purchase of a new multifamily residential property uses the market analysis to determine what cash flows they can expect to receive given the expected demand for units. The demand must be high enough to generate cash flows that provide a rate of return high enough to make the investment feasible.

In order to estimate the demand for multifamily housing units, it is necessary to understand recent population growth trends for the city. Then, it's important to consider the major industries in the market area and the forecasted growth for those industries over the next few years. You can then put this information together to forecast multifamily housing demand and compare that demand to the existing and proposed supply of multifamily units. This case study takes data about population and industrial activity in the Orlando, Florida region and analyzes supply and demand of multifamily residential units in the region.

Population Trends and Apartment Building Demand

Recent data from the U.S. Census Bureau and the Orlando Economic Development Commission lists the total population of the Orlando metro area at 2,387,138 (2016). Between 2015 and 2016, the population of the Orlando metro area grew by 2.6%. That made Orlando the fastest growing region in the United States. The Orlando Economic Development Commission estimates that population growth in the region since 2000 equates to a gain of 138 people per day. Population growth is mostly fueled by domestic migration. Americans moving to Orlando for retirement in warmer weather or for new career opportunities account for about 40% of the population increase. International migration (mainly from Central and South America) accounts for 34% of the increase in population. People have been moving to the Orlando area due to the region's comparative advantages (climate, entertainment and lifestyle, and economic growth). Without these advantages, Orlando would not be one of the fastest growing regions of the country.

With an average household size around 2.5, that means there are an estimated 954,855 households in the Orlando metropolitan area. Data from the American Consumer Survey indicates that about 43% of the population is renters. So, 43% of households would give an estimated demand of 410,588 multifamily units. In reality, not all renters live in multifamily units since many rent single-family homes. Therefore, it is necessary to estimate how many of those renters occupy multifamily units. A 2016 report from Fannie Mae estimated that there were 156,000 multifamily units in the Orlando metro area with a 5.75% vacancy rate. So, in 2016 there were around 147,030 occupied multifamily units (156,000 x (1-.0575) = 147,030). This means an estimated 35.8% of the households that are renters occupy multifamily units while the remaining 64.2% of renters occupy single-family homes.

Economic Trends and Multifamily Housing Demand

Employment data from the Bureau of Labor Statistics confirms that economic growth is driving the population growth in the Orlando metro area. In fact, job growth from 2015-2016 in Orlando was over twice the national average. A strong economy and growth in the number of jobs indicates that the population should continue to grow over the next few years unless there is a major shift to the national economy or a natural disaster. Furthermore, the job growth rate of 4.22% exceeded the population growth rate of 2.6%. If the major industries in Orlando continue to grow at this pace, more new workers will need to move into the region to fill these new jobs. So, forecasted population growth may be higher than the average of 2% seen over the past 10 years. It might be more appropriate to estimate population growth of at least 3% annually.

As with commodities traded on the market, housing prices continually fluctuate, sometimes with drastic changes over a short period of time. Availability is a huge factor affecting prices within a set region, such as in a specific suburb of a metropolitan area. Likewise, demand for homes in that market also plays into that price, which is why two nearly identical homes in different cities may sell for vastly different prices. When buying a home in a seller's market, limit your contingencies and make your offer as favorable to the seller as possible.

For houses and virtually anything else available for purchase, supply and demand play into the ultimate selling price. When an item is in short supply and many people want it, prices tend to rise. When the market is flooded with an item or there's no demand for it, prices fall. Sporting event ticket prices tend to rise when a team reaches the championship level, yet tickets to the same team's events a few years later, when the team isn't doing well, cost far less. Prices on holiday decor are another great example: At the peak of any holiday's shopping season, some shoppers are willing to pay a premium for the decor. Three days after the holiday, the leftover stock of these items is marked down to clearance prices due to little demand.

Housing supply and demand works in exactly the same way. Sometimes there are so many single-family homes available in the same region that there aren't enough buyers for all of them. In this housing oversupply, prices drop to draw more attention from potential buyers. A lowered price may influence an interested buyer to choose one home over a similar house in the same general area. Without a lowered price, a house may sit on the market for months due to the abundant number of similar homes for sale nearby at the same time.

On conclusion, property price change can be influenced by house buyers living need and land and house number supply factor, but any house buyer individual rational will influence his/her prerference property choice decision before he / she decides to choose what kinds properties or anywhere locations to live. So, house buyer individual psychological factor will influence his/her properties choices.

Case 6

Management science classical theory solves internet invention to raise smart phone sale number increases

Why does internet can influence smart mobile phone consumers' purchase desire? Has internet have direct relationship to influence smart mobile phone buyers' purchase desires ? Can the smart mobile phone talking product still attract phone buyers' preference choice, if it lacks internet function? Can internet raise smart phone sale number and create many mobile phone inventors and manufacturer occupations to raise GDP real GDP when smart phone buyers number and smart phone related occupation needs increase. I shall apply behavioral economic theory to attempt to explain the reasons how and why internet has direct relationship to influence smart mobile buyers' preference talking product choice in this traditional home telephone talking product market as below:

Is the internet putting up a barrier between people, even in bed? Does internet influence mobile phone consumers have not choose to buy because they are influenced to use mobiles when they use mobile to link internet to see any movies, or phones or news and influence their sleeping time in habit and they won't have nervous to work or learn on day time. We compulsively carry our smartphones with us wherever we go. The classroom, the bathroom, the bedroom, the outdoors — our phone is always in hand as if it were some magic self-defense tool capable of protecting us from all that is evil in the world. It all happened so fast. We didn't have the time to set any boundaries for smartphone usage, and now we find ourselves unable to save our relationships and form meaningful interactions with those dear to us.Smartphones are very useful in many circumstances. However, although not ruining your relationships per se, they can harm it in devious ways.

A smartphone is a modern day distraction that is so common, it's hardly noticed any more. It accompanies us wherever we go, demanding our attention multiple times a day. A phone call, a Facebook notification. We become irrevocably immersed in our digital lives, prioritizing the virtual world over anything else. Is it really that important to Instagram your dinner, rather than actually savoring it and sharing your impressions – or maybe a forkful of the dish – with the person next to you?Smartphones get in the way of our relationships, making it impossible for us to wholeheartedly devote our attention to the present moment. As a result, we lose many moments of wonder that are unique and never to be lived again. Addiction to smartphone usage is a common problem among adults worldwide. It manifests itself in the excessive usage of their phones, while engaged in other activities such as studying, driving, social gatherings and even sleeping. However, many people fail to realize that addiction to smartphone usage is a serious issue that can have a negative effect on the person's thoughts, behavior, tendencies, feelings, and sense of well-being. In particular, it can be a risk factor for depression, loneliness, anxiety and sleep disturbances. As per the Mental Health Foundation in the United Kingdom, people with depression experience an unhappy mood, loss of interest or pleasure, feelings of guilt or low self-worth, disturbed sleep or appetite, low energy, and poor concentration. Depressive and anxiety disorders are two main common disorders that are highly prevalent globally, as over 300 million people are estimated to suffer from depression, which is equivalent to 4.4% of the world's population. It is speculated that not only addiction to smartphone usage can affect one's mental and behavioral status, but also that those with mood disorders are more likely to become addicted to using their smartphones .

Numerous tools have been utilized in literature to assess the same phenomenon, but with different terms such as excessive smart phone usage, smartphone addiction, dependency on smart phones, internet addiction, problematic mobile phone usage, and so on. Remarkably, there was a tendency to use a non-pathological terminology, such as "Problematic Smartphone Use," rather than the term smartphone addiction. Addiction manifests itself in various forms such as preoccupation, tolerance, lack of control, withdrawal, mood modification, conflict, lies, excessive use and loss of interest. Several studies have found that women are more likely to develop an addiction to smartphone usage than men. This was viewed as a positive way for people to stay connected in social relationships. One study clarified that women like to show affection to their families using their smartphones while men use phones for efficiency and practicality . Though there are several studies on this topic, no study has proven this connection so far. Smartphone addiction has been found to be correlated with various physical and psychological issues, as indicated in a number of studies that tested this relationship among various age groups. For example, one study found that people with depression, social anxiety and loneliness had different uses for their smartphones compared to others. People with social anxiety made fewer outgoing calls, as well as, fewer text messages than those without social anxiety. It was reported that high levels of smartphone addiction were correlated with low self-esteem, loneliness, depression and shyness.

Although, internet can bring smart mobile phone users to spend sleeping time to use this kind of mobile product to watch movies, watch TV, listen music, social media communication, searching etc. non-talking communication behaviors. It seems that internet may influence smart phone users to change their phone purchase choice to buy the kind common mobile product more. But, in behavioral economic view, internet can bring smart mobile phone product has more attractive strengths to influence common mobile phone kind product users to chooce to use smart mobile phone products in preference. Internet can also bring these positive emotion to persuade the common mobile users to choose to use them.

Convenient applying: Any smart phone users can apply smart phone to link to internet to replace home computers to link to internet to watch movies, watch TV, listen music, social media communication, searching etc. non-talking communication behaviors in anywhere and any time conveniently. It is one kind of small size and light talking communication tool, but it can also help any mobile users to apply smart phone product to apply internet to do the same computer tasks in any time and any places. Hence, smart mobile can bring many computer users to feel that they can apply computer to do similar internet search behaviors at home. Convenient internet search function is one attract function to influence traditional computer users to choose to apply smart phone tools to replace computers tools to apply internet to search information, news, watch TV, movie, lisen music etc. social media communication behaviors at homes. When they bring smart phone to any where, then they can apply this tool to click to internet to do the same computer and internet link tasks in order to enjoy their entertainment needs. So, they do not need to apply computer tool to link to internet to enjoy their visal entertainment at homes. They can bring smart phone to go to anywhere to link to internet to enjoy their visal entertainment in any time conveniently. So, smart phone can be replaced to home computer tool to solve any visal entertainment enjoyers' needs.

● Internet brings smart phone users to feel more visal entertainment enjoyment

The Internet has revolutionized direct communication, lead to the digitization of books and film, as well as made convenience even more important. Companies have developed strategies that capitalize on the growing desire for easily accessible goods and services in only a few mouse clicks. As technology grows increasingly local and more connected to all aspects of the customer purchasing process, small business owners need to be more efficient in how they target their markets. Understanding why convenience plays such a large role in the purchasing process is vital in growing a successful business. Here are five trends that have popped up in recent years as businesses looked for ways to help their customers take advantage of well-timed opportunities. Internet can bring more attract to smart phone users, instead of visal enjoyment needs, the reasons may include as below:

1. Prior Consumer Knowledge

In today's digital world, consumers are looking for retail solutions which allow them to maximize their free-time and to stretch their disposable income. Due to this economic climate, small businesses which are able to provide their customer with a more convenient experience than a large retailer, are cashing in. H.M Cole, a custom clothier, offers its customers an entire planned wardrobe for the upcoming year after an hour's consultation. Other convenience services such as Trunk Club and Stitch Fix, personalized styling sites for men and women respectively, take that one step further in creating a complete look. These levels of convenience take a simple fitting and turn it into a way for consumers to spend less time deciding outfits, and more time doing other things they value.

2. Direct-to Store Delivery

Due to the "larger-than-life" nature of big box stores, they have begun to develop strategies which combat the convenience of a smaller retailer. The newest trend among these chains is to offer direct-to store delivery. Shoppers are able to find what they are looking for online, and purchase directly on the site. Rather than having to wait the 3-5 days for delivery, chains are making their purchases available (sometimes at discounted rates) for pick up at their local store. Essentially, customers are taking part in shopping services where the store physically groups together the inventory, saving the individual time in their purchases.

3. Personalized Billing, Shipping Info

Customer profiles across frequently visited webpages allow for consumers to not only keep their billing information in one place, but also have access to similar products or content. Businesses are able to not only track purchases, but to specifically target an individual with the information provided for convenience sake. A user does not usually choose to re-enter billing or shipping information on a site they frequent, and so by saving this information, a company is removing an obstacle that might otherwise influence the purchase.

4. Time is Money

Fast food and drive-thru options have changed the world's nutritional demands, creating a society of cheap convenience foods. Although the nutritional value of these highly-processed foods is lacking, the demand for them has been on the rise across the globe. While these types of businesses are growing at a record rate, the pressure to remain affordable and convenient has driven them online.

Some innovative restaurant chains have transitioned to online ordering which provide an easy, personalized interface for their customers to select and buy all from the website portal. A restaurant receives the order digitally, packages the food, and then sends it out to delivery, often for an additional fee. Both Google and Amazon , as well as many startups, have launched services that deliver meals and groceries to your home. Time has shown that customers are willing to spend a little more for the convenience of having food arrive at their doorstep.

5. Subscription Services

Another recent convenience service trend is through subscription services. This can include streaming goods such as TV shows, movies, audio books, or music tracks. Companies charge their customers a fee to have access to a database of content whenever, wherever they want. Some providers have included commercials as a means to generate more income. Other subscription services include coffee of the month clubs, or deliver gift boxes. These companies charge a monthly (or yearly) subscription fee and compile a box of themed goodies for their customers.While some very big companies have struggled to make convenience a larger part of their customers' experiences, many small businesses that offer niche products and services have an advantage in this area. The Internet is helping them to level the playing field in a way. It provides a platform for small businesses to capitalize on the demand for goods by using convenience to win fans and new customers.

On conclusion, internet can bring smart phone users to do any activities when they need to apply computer tools at home in any time and anywhere. So, internet has direct relationship to persuade mobile phone or computer users to choose to buy mobiles for communication uses or internet uses in preference nowadays as well as internet can bring the different kinds of new or unique mobile phones design needs increase to achieve the creating mobile phone inventors and mobile phone manufacturers occupations need. So, it seems that internet can influence mobile phone product's occupations needs and mobile phone consumers number increase to raise real GDP growth to the smart phone maufacturing and sale country really.

Reference

Bigne, Enrique (2005). The impact of internet user shopping patterns and demographics on consumer mobile buying.

Falk, Louis, K. et. al (2005) " E-commerce and consumer's expectations: What makes a website work". Journal of website promotion, 1(1), 65-75.

Parasuraman, A., Zeithaml, V.A. and Berry L.L. (1988) SERVQUAL: A multiple-item scale for measuring consumer perceptions of
service quality. Journal of retailing, 64, 12-40.

Case 7

GAME THOERY SOLUTION IBM AND MICROSOFT COMPUTER LARGE COMPANIES COOPERATION MANAGEMENT PROBLEM CASE

Economics is just as much about consumer and producer behavior as it is about finance or the allocation of resources. With that in mind, game theory will explain one of the most fundamental tools economists use to frame competitive decision making. It provides a systematic approach to decision-making in competitive environments and a framework for the study of conflict.

Game theory solves the Prisoner's social criminal behaviors

Two small-time criminals are out breaking into cars, stealing what they can. They are working together in the same area of town. Fortunately, they get caught and booked down at the station. The detective goes in to question them separately and offers them both the same deal: they can either confess or stay silent. Their punishment will be determined by what action they take and what action the other perp takes. Here's what could happen:

a) If both perps confess, they each get 3 years.

b) If both perps stay silent, they each get 1 year.

c) If perp #1 stays silent and perp #2 confesses, perp #2 serves NO time and perp #1 serves 10 years.

d) If perp #2 stays silent and perp #1 confesses, perp #1 serves NO time and perp #2 serves 10 years.

So, if you were perp #1, what would you do? You could stay quiet and count on only getting one year, hoping that your friend stays quiet as well, and you'll both only serve 1 year. But, what if you admit to being involved and they admit being involved as well, then you'll both get 3 years. Or, what if you stay silent but your friend admits? Then you'll get 10 years; that wouldn't be good! Well, it is if your friend stays quiet.

The lesson to be learned from the prisoner's dilemma described above is how difficult it is to make an optimal decision when two competitors - and that's what these two perps are right now - can't collaborate. Typically, the economic man (or woman) is someone who makes decisions based on their own self-interest and chooses that which maximizes their own benefits. The entire idea behind game theory is that the result of your decision isn't known to you until you find out what your friend (or competitor) is going to do, so you have to make the best decision you can based on the information you have.

Game Theory in Real Life

We know how game theory works in a fictional situation that would never really happen, but what about how game theory applies to real life? Well, we can talk about that, too. Think about any strategic decision a business might make. The success or failure of that decision may very well depend on how the competition reacts. Perhaps a fast food restaurant wants to build a new location on the corner of a popular intersection. They complete their analysis of traffic flow, demand, other options in the area, etc., and ultimately decide it's a good idea. Then, once construction begins, another restaurant opens up a new location across the street, with a new building plan that includes drive-through ordering. What does our first restaurant do now?

Technology marketing cooperative strategy

Future when the thinking capabilities of computers approach our own is quickly coming into view. Raid process in coming decades will bring about machines with human –level intelligence capable of speech and reasoning, with a myriad of contributions to economics, politics and warcraft. The birth of true artificial intelligence will profoundly affect humankind's future. In our future technological development market, what it will bring much influences to economy. I shall indicate these several aspects, they may include as below:

On artificial intelligent invention brings high unemployment to low skill employees aspect, from the time the last artificial intelligence break through was reached in the last 1940s, scientists around the world have looked for ways of this " artificial intelligence" to improve technology, raising efficiency and productivity beyond what even the most sophisticated of today's artificial intelligence programs can achieve. Even now, research is ongoing to better understand what the new AI programs will be able to do, when remaining within the intelligence such as human brain. Most AI programs currently programmed have been limited primarily to making simple decisions or performing simple operations on relatively small amounts of data.

AI technological invention will bring much contribution to influence our future economic development. It had unique characteristics to compare common machines and it can help many industries to raise efficiency, productivity and improve performance as well as consumer individual self use. Such as the network is not taught to understand prose in any human sense. Instead, during its training phase, it adjusts the internal connections in its simulated neural networks to best anticipate the next word. It can be applied to read any article and understand any meaning to write any article as same to authors' mind and writing ability. For example, in the future, any one entered the first few sentences of any article, you are reading, the algorithm spewed out two paragraphs that sounded liked a freshman's effort to recall the gist of an introductory lecture on machine learning during which she was daydreaming. The output contains all the right words and phrases , not bad. So, (AI) technology can be applied to become just one more example of programs that do things thought to be uniquely human playing the real-time strategy game, translating text, making personal recommendations for books and movies, recognizing people in images and videos. But with the invention, of deep neural networks and the massive computational of the tech industry, computers improved until their outputs to longer appeared . In the future, algorithms can best humans, (AI) can help human to do any things in possible. Then, our society will encounter one automobile machine working environment. Does (AI) innovation will low skill employees lose their jobs because robotic can replace to any human to do simple jobs in any industries.

Whether machines can become sentient matters for ethical reasons. If computers experience life through their own senses, they cease to be purely a means to an end determined by their usefulness to us humans. Then our society will have many jobs which are needed to be worked by human, due to (AI) or robotic invention, it can replace human to do many simple jobs, e.g. factory manufacturing jobs, warehouse deliver jobs, public transportation , e.g. tram, train, ferry, underground train, bus etc. driving tasks, they are replaced by robotic auto driving, even pilot flying job will be also replaced to drive air planes by (AI) driving on sky impossible. Although, (AI) can help businesses to raise efficiency, increase productivity and improve performance, but it also bring these jobs to be replaced by (AI) and it will cause many people lose jobs when (AI) is invented to be applied in popular in our future societies. On business benefits aspect, (AI) can bring working efficiency and productivity improvement, but it can also bring unemployment ratio raises as the same time when employers accept to apply (AI) to replace human to any simple or difficult tasks.

So, we need to limit or prohibit (AI) invention to exceed human's extent in possible. I mean that we do not need to limit to invent any (AI) skill, but we need to concern human need to work in the same time. If (AI) was real replaced to do any simple jobs in any industries, then there are many low skill workers , such as factory workers, clean workers, drivers ,even high skill workers, such as lawyer, teacher, pilot. They will lose their jobs in possible. So, how to invent (AI) technology will influence our future global employment chance to provide us to continue to work in any organizations. So, (AI) will may bring high unemployment ratio, if it is applied to any low skill , even high skill jobs aspects to different industries in global.

On conclusion , in economist view, technology market development must need, such as (AI) invention because it can help any industries to raise efficiency, productivity and improve performance, but we need to know how it can be applied to avoid human to lose jobs, due to (AI) is replaced to do their tasks for any industries in possible. Whether (AI) invention can create jobs or bring job lose? (AI) scientists must need to consider how to invent their skill to be applied to which tasks aspect if they hope human won't lose many jobs to do in future one day.

● How to apply robotic to raise efficiency and productivity and improving performance for manufacture as well as bringing long term productive economic benefit to manufacturers?

It is one good question. Can scientists only concentrate on researching artificial intelligent for raising productivity, efficiency and improving performance to businesses aspect, so neglecting on research other scientific researching aspects? Technological marketing economy is as a play between independent individual subjects. However, it has also become clear that the notion of play has to be interpreted within a different framework than that of classical functionalism. In mainstream classical economics, interaction or exchange is understood as the effect of the ends-means rationally of individuals. Smith's sympathy –based view of man and society avoids this functionalistic reduction of interaction and exchange. For example, the utilitarian or functional aspect of , the social process of producing and distributing wealth through free exchange, is in Smith's view on part of the value and belief system which people in ordered and prosperous societies employ to give sense and meaning to their experiences.

Hence, in our business society, technology can bring marketing economic change to be better. One free technology marketing economic society must have these advantages to bring to influence our living, such as below:

It interprets and explains improving social processes of producing and distributing to business, such as (AI) skill invention , it can help businesses to improve performance and efficiency and productivities for their manufacturing aim only, but (AI) ought not be applied to replace to do all low skill workers' jobs in any positions in any factories or warehouses. So, any employers ought not dismiss all workers and they are replaced by all robotics. They will need to consider overall economic benefit. I mean that avoiding low skill workers unemployment ratio raises. For example, one factory can still keep 50% workers and 50% robotics to cooperate to work together. Because some human workers can be such as assistants to do any simple tasks in factory every teams. Human workers can discover any errors to let manager to know in order to improve in their cooperation process with robotics. So, human workers and robotics cooperation , it is more efficient manufacturing method to compare any manufacturing process is needed to finish from robotics only in any future factory or warehouse working environment. So, robotics and human workers cooperation can bring the most efficient production and distribution benefits to future manufacturers in any factories or warehouses because human can help robotics to find any error in order to improve. Otherwise, if the factory or warehouse has only all robotics to work. Although, they may bring raising productivities or improving performance and efficiencies. But they can not know whether how to improve their errors or revises their every time productive performance to be better every day. SO, the most efficient manufacturing method is that human workers and robotics cooperate to work together in any factories or warehouses.

On innovation and information economic influence aspect, one of the most important topics in economics is the economics of information. Information includes things as varied as e-mail, and even the text book you are reading. Information is a very different kind of commodity from things like pizza and shoes because information is expensive to produce , but cheap to reproduce. Because of the unusual nature of information, it is subject to market failure, so we need to develop different kinds of public politics to regulate it, the law of " intellectual property".

We are encountering the essence of economic development is innovation and that monopolists are in fact of innovation in a capitalist economy. What does the economics of information mean ? Who do we need to develop information economy? Modern economics emphasizes the special problems involved in the economics of information. Information is a fundamentally different commodity from normal goods. Because information is costly to produce , but cheap to reproduce, markets in information are subject to serve market failures.

For the production of software program industry example, the windows software, developing this program took several years and cost Microsoft many money of dollars. You can purchase a legal copy for $5. The same phenomenon is at work in pharmaceutical, entertainment and other areas where much of the value of a good comes from the information it contains. In each of these areas, the research and development to software on the product may be an expensive process that takes years. But once, the information is recorded on paper, in a computer or on a compact disc, it can be reproduced and used by a second person essentially for free.

The inability of firms to capture the full monetary value of their invention is called inappropriability. Inventions are not fully appropriable because other firms may imitate an invention, in which case the other firms may derive some of the benefits of the inventive investments. Sometimes, imitators may drive down the price of the new product, in which case consumers would get some of the rewards. Information consumers can earn these benefits when the value of an invention to all consumers and producers is many times the appropriable private return to the inventor (the monetary value of the invention to the inventor).

However, information is expensive to produce but cheap to reproduce. To the extent the rewards to invention are inappropriable, we would expect private research and development to be underfunded, with the most significant underinvestment in basic research because that is the least appropriable kind of information. The inappropriability and high social return on research can lead most governments to subsidize basic research in the fields of health and science and to provide special incentives for other creative activities. Thus, special laws governing patents, copyrights, business and trade secrets and electronic media create intellectual property rights. The purpose is to give the owner special protection against the material's being copied and used .by others without compensation to the owner or original creator.

On the Internet information economic market influence hand, inventions that improve communications are hardly limited to the modern age. But the rapid growth of electronic storage, access and transmission of information highlights of providing incentives for creating new information. Many new information technologies have large sunk costs but virtually zero marginal costs. With the low cost of electronic information systems like the internet, it is technologically possible to make the large amounts of information available to everyone, everywhere, at close to zero marginal cost. Perfect competition is nowadays different e-commerce internet information business competitive feature, and any e-commerce merchants can not survive here because a price equal to a zero marginal cost will yield zero revenues and therefore no viable firms.

Hence, the economics of the information economy highlights the conflict between efficiency and incentives. On the one hand, all information ,might be provided free of charge, e.g. free e-book download, e-song download e-movie download from internet. Free provisions of information looks economically efficient because the price would thereby be equal to the marginal cost, which is zero. But a zero price on intellectual property would destroy the profits and therefore reduce the incentives to produce new books from authors, movies and songs from creators would earn little rewards from their creative activity. But with the costs reproduction and transmission so much lower for electronic information than for traditional information, so the future any electronic publishing industry 's products, e.g. e-books, e-songs , e-music, e-movies prices will be lower than traditional paper books, pack of songs and movies price, either consumers go to shops to buy them or consumers pay visa card to enter websites to buy any e-books , songs, e-music , e-movies from internet channel. Then, it will cause these traditional publishing and entertainment industries' competition to be raised because these e-publishers or e-entertainment can reduce their price to sell from their websites when their costs are nearly to zero. Hence, information technology can raise competition to the traditional publishing and entertainment industries. The traditional paper book, music, movie business merchants need to any authors or creators to help them to create any unique movies, songs, paper books to sell from their shops and they need to ensure their authors or music , movie creators won't give these creative book, song, movie products to any e-music, e-publisher, e-movie merchants to sell from their websites absolutely.

On conclusion, information technology influence any music, publish, movie creative product competitive raising to the traditional paper book publishers, music or movie publishers when many book publishers or music or movie creators choose e-commerce to replace traditional shop visiting sale method. So ' it is possible to influence overall publishing and music and movie creative industries will change to e-commence consumption model. Then the traditional book and music and movie visiting stores will disappear and the online websites to these merchants will increase and their price also will reduce in global e-publishing and e-creative product consumption environment. So, information technology will bring some traditional store visiting number decreases and online merchant e-store number increases and consumers can pay less price to buy these creative products from internet.

New trade game theory explains IBM and Micro software both compaines cooperative advantages
New trade theory (NTT) suggests that a critical factor in determining international patterns of trade are the very substantial economies of scale and network effects that can occur in key industries.
These economies of scale and network effects can be so significant that they outweigh the more traditional theory of comparative advantage. In some industries, two countries may have no discernible differences in opportunity cost at a particular point in time. But, if one country specialises in a particular industry then it may gain economies of scale and other network benefits from its specialisation.
Another element of new trade theory is that firms who have the advantage of being an early entrant can become a dominant firm in the market. This is because the first firms gain substantial economies of scale meaning that

new firms can't compete against the incumbent firms. This means that in these global industries with very large economies of scale, there is likely to be limited competition, with the market dominated by early firms who entered, leading to a form of monopolistic competition.

Monopolistic competition is an important element of New Trade Theory, it suggests that firms are often competing on branding, quality and not just simple price. It explains why countries can both export and import designer clothes. This means that the most lucrative industries are often dominated in capital-intensive countries, who were the first to develop these industries. Therefore, being the first firm to reach industrial maturity gives a very strong competitive advantage. (some may say unfair advantage) New trade theory also becomes a factor in explaining the growth of globalisation. It means that poorer, developing economies may struggle to ever develop certain industries because they lag too far behind the economies of scale enjoyed in the developed world. This is not due to any intrinsic comparative advantage, but more the economies of scale the developed firms already have.

Examples of New Trade Theory

•Specialisation of IT in Silicon Valley – the US. Hewlett and Packard started their computer business. Success attracted more IT firms to that area. Not because of any particular intrinsic benefit but new firms start to get the network benefits of being around other IT setups.'

•Globalisation has led to increased variety for consumers. The proliferation of brand clothing labels. Firms competing in the model of monopolistic competition and heavy branding. Neither UK or Italy has a particular comparative advantage in producing clothes, but consumers are attracted to brand image of Italian and British fashion labels.

Moral hazard influences to Macrosoft or Microcorp and IBM software cooperational success problem

Moral hazard is when one party can take risks knowing the other party will bear the consequences. It describes the risk present when two parties don't have the same information about actions that take place after an agreement is in place. The situation creates a temptation to ignore the moral implications of a decision: doing what benefits you most instead of doing what is right.

Example of Moral Hazard in Insurance

Moral hazard is a term that originated in the insurance industry and spread to the financial sphere. To illustrate the concept, imagine you rent a car and opt for the maximum insurance coverage possible. Damaging the vehicle does not have significant negative consequences for you, because the insurance company pays for repairs—or a replacement car—if something happens.

The insurance company uses statistics to estimate how likely the vehicle is to suffer damage, and they price their services accordingly. You pay much less for insurance than it would cost to repair a car because, in most cases, the insurance company won't have to pay for any repairs. But there are times when you might have an unfair information advantage over your insurance company. That's where moral hazard comes in.

You plan to drive into the mountains on rough, narrow roads. So, you get the most generous insurance coverage possible, and you don't worry about bouncing over rocks or scratching the paint in thick brush along the side of the road. You might even have a perfectly good car available at home, but there's no way you're going to drive your vehicle up that road—so you rent a car and buy insurance. The low cost of insurance means you have no incentive to protect the car you rented, but the insurance company doesn't know you're driving it under such conditions.

Moral hazard happens when you have an incentive to take risks that somebody else will pay for. You get to do whatever brings you the greatest potential benefit, and you don't suffer the consequences. In this example, the insurance company bears the risk: the cost of repairing or even replacing the car. The more insulated you are from risk, the more temptation you face.

Examples of Moral Hazard in Lending

Moral hazard became a significant factor during (and after) the financial crisis that began in 2007. The concept can apply to both lenders and borrowers.

Lenders were eager to approve loans before the mortgage crisis. Some mortgage brokers encouraged "subprime" borrowers to lie on loan applications, or they altered documents to make it appear that borrowers were able to afford loans that they really couldn't afford. For example, sometimes they reported inaccurate income numbers or the brokers did not require documentation that would demonstrate a borrower's ability to repay the loan.

Why would lenders hand out money when they don't know if the borrower can afford the payments—especially if they have to commit fraud to get the loans approved? In many cases, the lenders were only originating, or selling, the loans. After approving and funding loans, lenders would sell the loans to investors, who eventually suffered the losses. In other words, the lender took little or no risk. But lenders had an incentive to keep making new loans because that's how originators generate revenue.

When things turned sour, lawmakers and the public got scared. They worried that if major banks collapsed (some of them were loan originators, while others held risky investments), they would bring down the U.S. economy—not to mention the global economy. Because these banks were considered "too big to fail," the U.S. government provided funding to help some of them to weather the economic storm. If those banks suffered significant losses, the government promised to protect deposits (in some cases through the FDIC). Of course, taxpayers fund the U.S. government, so the taxpayers were ultimately bailing out the banks. The moral hazard was the lenders and investment banks taking risks that had consequences not for themselves, but for taxpayers and others.

Borrowers

Moral hazard can occur in almost any agreement, whether it's an informal understanding or a formal contract. If one party has the opportunity to benefit from taking "risks"—while risking almost nothing—moral hazard is at play.

During the financial crisis, as millions of homeowners struggled to pay their mortgages and loan defaults skyrocketed, government programs offered relief. People could avoid foreclosure thanks to money and guarantees from the U.S. government.

The moral hazard in these cases was that borrowers, increasingly underwater on their home loans, would be tempted to walk away from their mortgage rather than repay it. Such an action would put risk back onto the lender. The hazard is that the borrower no longer had an incentive to do the right thing—to pay back the mortgage as agreed.

Hence, such as moral hazard applies to Macrosoft or Microcorp and IBM software cooperational case . If Macrosoft and Microsorp and IBM do not decide to co-operate to help themselves to expand their software strengths to achieve the aim to improve their software quality and feature and function, then they can not bring any software innovation to let future software users to raise any new softwares invention or improvement useful benefits. Then, global software market can not be improved to let any software users to raise high techological software products choices number.

Because they are competitors, they won't hope themselves softwares' quality, feature and function and improvement are worse to compare other softwares companies among them. So, global software users will have moral hazard to enjoy any kinds of new softwares products invention in short time. But, if they can cooperate to buy and sell themselves both shares, then they both will be another softwares owners, they won't hope the another software company loses many software customers because itself new software inventions to attack the another software company. They must hope themselves any new software invention products , they can still attract many new software products customers together. Then, global software users won't have moral hazard to enjoy any new software invention products in short time, because they must cooperate to help themselve to improve their any new softwares ' qualities , features and functions in order to they can have many software customers share in these software market when they are global large software firms.

What are Principal-Agent Problems to Microsoft and IBM both large computer companies cooperation?

For example, a company's stock investors, as part-owners, are principals who rely on the company's chief executive officer (CEO), as their agent, to carry out a strategy in their best interests. That is, they want the stock to increase in price or pay a dividend, or both. If the CEO opts instead to plow all the profits into expansion or pay big bonuses to managers, the principals may feel they have been let down by their agent. There are a number of remedies for the principal-agent problem, and many of them involve clarifying expectations and monitoring results. The principal is generally the only party who can or will correct the problem.

Understanding the Principal-Agent Problem

The principal-agent problem has become a standard factor in political science and economics. The theory was developed in the 1970s by Michael Jensen of Harvard Business School and William Meckling of the University of Rochester. In a paper published in 1976, they outlined a theory of an ownership structure designed to avoid what they defined as agency cost and its cause, which they identified as the separation of ownership and control.The trend has been towards contracts with the agent that link compensation directly to performance measurements set by the principal.

This separation of control occurs when a principal hires an agent, The principal delegates a degree of control and the right to make decisions to the agent. But the principal retains ownership of the assets and the liability for any losses.

Factoring in Agency Costs

Logically, the principal cannot constantly monitor the agent's actions. The risk that the agent will shirk a responsibility, make a poor decision, or otherwise act in a way that is contrary to the principal's best interest, can be defined as agency costs. Additional agency costs can be incurred while dealing with problems that arise from an agent's actions. Agency costs are viewed as a part of transaction costs.

Agency costs may also include the expenses of setting up financial or other incentives to encourage the agent to act in a particular way. Principals are willing to bear these additional costs as long as the expected increase in the return on the investment from hiring the agent is greater than the cost of hiring the agent, including the agency costs.

Examples of the Principal-Agent Problem

The principal-agent problem can crop up in many day-to-day situations beyond the financial world. A client who hires a lawyer may worry that the lawyer will wrack up more billable hours than are necessary. A homeowner may disapprove of the City Council's use of taxpayer funds. A home buyer may suspect that a realtor is more interested in a commission than in the buyer's concerns. In all of these cases, the principal has little choice in the matter. An agent is necessary to get the job done.However, there are ways to resolve the principal-agent problem.

Solutions to the Principal-Agent Problem

The onus is on the principal to create incentives for the agent to act as the principal wants. Consider the first example, the relationship between shareholders and a CEO. The shareholders can take action before and after hiring a manager to overcome some risk. First, they can write the manager's contract in a way that aligns the incentives of the manager with the incentives of the shareholders. The principals can require the agent to regularly report results to them. They can hire outside monitors or auditors to track information. In the worst case, they can replace the manager.

Contract Clauses

In recent years, the trend has been towards employment contracts that connect compensation as closely as possible with performance measurements. For managers of businesses, incentives include performance-based awards of stock or stock options, profit-sharing plans, or directly linking management pay to stock price. At its root, it's the same principle as tipping for good service. Theoretically, tipping aligns the interests of the customer, or the principal, and the agent, or the waiter. Their priorities are now aligned and are focused on good service.

Hence, such as this IBM and microsoft large both companies, if they hope to cooperate , they need to solve which company can have more management authority and which company can have more share owming or investing authory. If IBM can have more management authority to control their both companies, but IBM has less shares number to Microsoft, e.g. IBM has 30 % shares to Microsoft, whether IBM ought earn more profit or less profit to 30% profits from Microsoft, if IBM have more management authory, but IBM can not cooperate to Microsoft to assist it to raise more computer buyers number. So, agent problem will cause IBM and Microsoft cooperation more easily together in nowadays computer market. But, if IBM can help Microsoft to increase computer buyers number after IBM participates to manage Microsoft's internal organizational management , then IBM can increase Microsoft computer buyers number in long time. Then, their cooperation can be more success, it means that their principle and agent problem will solve between them.

Management Science Dependency Theory Solves Macrosoft and IBM software cooperational success method

● Macrosoft or Microcorp and IBM software cooperational strategy
What is information technologic game strategy? How and why information technological game strategy can influence economic growth? I shall explain as below:

Nowadays, Macrosoft and Microcorp are the global information technological big companies. They own much market share in global information technological industry. Whether what factors influence they can still be global information technological products leaders. Why does computer software consumers still choose their products to compare other software products in preference? I suppose that Macrosoft and Microcorp, their hypothetical any software games have developed a clever new computer game that is certain to be very popular. Although Microcorp have the unique competitive advantage with its own software game engineers and compete against Macrosoft, but it can so it cheaper and better if it can hire any Macrosoft's software game engineers. So, in economic view, it needs to pay high salary (higher cost) to hire Macrosoft's engineers (labor), but Macrosoft's engineers can help Microcorp to invent any new kinds of software games to compete Macrosoft. Although, Microsorp needs to pay higher labor cost, but when it can raise its any software games' design and game playing methods to attract any game players. Then, these new and exciting software games can help it can bring many game entertainment players and then it can sell cheaper price to raise more attractive effort to win its competitor (Macrosoft). So, higher software game designing engineers (skill labor), their game designing effort will be the major factor to influence any one information technological companies in success. If one software designing company can employ one high software game designing effort profession to help it to design any kinds of attractive software games. Although, it may pay high salary (labor cost), but it have much chance to attract many software game buyers to compare that if it pays less salary to employ one poor game software designing profession. Because the poor software game designing profession may need to spend long time to research how to design any kinds of attractive game software to excite game players' playing desires in this playing software game industry market. Long time research to the poor software game designer may be one none any reward to compensate to the software game designing firm when it needs to pay long time salary to employ him. Otherwise, if the software game designing firm can accept to pay higher salary to the higher software game designer, he will have higher chance to help it to design any more attractive software games to influence game players' playing game entertainment desires. So, any software game designing companies their game designers (labor) must be the major factor to influence their business succeeds or fails in this software game entertainment market.

On the employing method hand, Microcorp can choose to include in its contracts with its software engineers that from working for another Macrosoft software company for a certain period of time if they resign from Macrosoft. A move such as this is sometimes called a preeptive move. Its propose is to alter its rivals' payoffs in order to alter their employing strategies. Preemptive moves are usually costly (high slaary), and this one is no exception. In its employment contracts makes Macrosoft a less attractive to let its old game software engineers want to leave their current employer, such as Macrosoft. As a result, Macrosoft must pay its software game designing engineers above the going market salary if it hopes their employment contracts can be continue between Macrosoft and its software game engineers.

Should Macrosoft must need to decide how to react. It can choose to fight Microcorp by aggressively advertising its game, which is costly high, but gives it a larger market share in the game player entertainment market, when Macrosoft had any one profession game software engineer(s) leave(s) his company and he/they change(s) to the another Microcorp software game designing company to work, or it can forego the expense of an advertisement campaign and simply share the market 50/50 with its major competitor, Microcorp to be partners.

Their competition has close relationship to influence economic growth because it will have many game players number to be increase if they can cooperate to be partners in success when they can design any new kinds of software game products to satisfy software game players' entertainment feeling. Otherwise, if they can not be one good partners and they only consider their every business benefits and neglect themselves business benefits. Then, their software playing games sale price can either to be reduced in order to attract any software game players when their software games can not be designed to have much new playing methods to attract many game players. Consequently, the GDP income to this software game entertainment market must reduce because any kinds of entertainment software games prices are reduced as well as the game players number is also decreasing. Due to they are the major software entertainment game suppliers in global. Any game players will only choose either Microcorp or Macrosoft to buy their any kinds of entertainment software game products to play majorly. So, their software game manufacturing and sale number must influence global GDP income increases or decreases in macro economy view. It implies that any countries technological software game industry's GDP income will depend on these both Microcorp and Macrosoft software game's cooperation relationship whether they have good or bad cooperation relationship. If their cooperation relationship is good, then they can manufacture high quality and attractive entertainment software games as well as raising sale price and exciting many game players' entertainment desires to achieve the increase to game players number aim more easily.

How to achieve their cooperation relationship more easier. I suppose that, in the software game entertainment industry, over its lifetime, the computer game will generate $500,000 in new income (income minus production cost) for all the firms producing it or its clones. Macrosoft must pay its software engineers an additional $100,000 to get them to agree to accept a contract containing an anticompetition clause. It costs Microcorp $100,000 to develop the software if it can hire Macrosoft's engineers and $200,000 otherwise. Aggressive advertising costs Macrosoft $70,000 and has the effect of giving it a 80% market share if it restricts its engineers' employment and a 72% market share if it does not. So, the fall in total market share is caused by the fact that without some of Macrosoft's advertisements. If however, Macrosoft passively acquiesces to Microcorp's entry and shares the market, then both firms can still achieve a 50% market share fairly. Hence, they must need to achieve 50/50 market share if they hope to achieve the cooperation relationship in success. Otherwise, they will not achieve cooperation relationship in success.

However, the spending advertisement factor will also their cooperation chance in success. For example, it would be more realistic to recast the Software Game as one in which Macrosoft chooses how much to spend on advertising with sales depending continuously on the amount spent. Other examples of continuous cooperation choices may include: the productive capacity of an electrical power plant; the salary to offer a prospective employee; or the insurance premium to charge a prospective policyholder. So, the amount to any of these expenditure factor will influence whether they will decide to cooperate to sell their software games products in global game entertainment market.

How and why Macrosoft and Microcorp's cooperation can influence global economic growth? It is significant that Macrosoft and Microcorp both technological software game designing companies are global the largest firms, they are doing international software game trade business to many countries and they have large market share in the software entertainment game sale market. Aside from trade based on technological gaps and software game product cycles, software game entertainment industry is dynamic in nature or game players' entertainment taste will change any time in completely static in nature. That is, given the nation's game players' playing taste and game entertainment factor, such as game playing designing technological method and game player individual playing game taste both. We proceeded to determine the nation's comparative advantage and the gains from the different kinds of entertainment software game designing supply factor and the game player individual game taste changing factor. So, any nation's software game players number will depend on these both factors to influence whether their number will either increase or decrease in the year in this global software game entertainment market. However, these factors can be changed by time, technology usually can improve any software game playing methods and game player individual playing taste will also change any time. As a result, the nation's comparative advantage also changes over time, such as when the nation has many game players lose their interest to buy any software games to play, then the nation ought not only consider how to develop its software entertainment game in the technological industry, it is right time to research any other new technological industries to develop if it still hopes its GDP income can rise in the technological industry overall aspect. Such as dynamic trade theory is still in its infancy. However, our comparative statics analysis can carry us a long way in analyzing the effect on international trade resulting from changes in factor technology, and tastes over time, such as entertainment software game case.

The growth of factors of production will also influence the software game entertainment industry development, through time, a nation's population usually grows and with its size of its labor force , such as China and India. Similarly, by utilizing part of its resources to produce capital equipment, e.g. India needs to utilize its technological resources, technological engineers and technological material can need to be used to manufacture either new software game products or computers. But, its technological resources will be shortage (both labor and technological material). So, many technological companies choose to apply more technological material and technological engineers to use much time and money to manufacture any new software game products. Then, these labor and material resources will be reduced to be spent time and material to manufacture any new computer products in the year. In this technological industry case, capital refers to all the man-made means of production, such as machinery, factories, communication and education and training of labor force, all of which greatly enhance the nation's ability to produce either computer products or software game products. So, the national will also continue to assume that it can experiencing economic growth is producing two commodities, such as software game and computer both kinds of technological products under the constant returns to scale. So, if India can not raise the rapid technical process to skill labor and supply technological material supplying number to satisfy to manufacture the enough software game and computer products to supply them to sell to any countries' playing game players and computer users every month. Then, its technological industry will lose many clients, due to it can not supply enough software games and computers number to sell to any countries.

Several empirical studies have indicated that most the increase in real per capita income in technological industrial nations is due to technical progress and much less to capital accumulation. However, the analysis of technical progress is much more complex than the analysis of factor growth because there are several definitions and types of technical progress, and they can take place at different rates in the production of either or both commodities, such as software game and computer.

Technical progress is usually classified into neutral, labor saving , or capital saving. All technical progress , regardless of its types reduces the amount of both labor and capital required to produce any given level of output. So, if India could have good technical progress to raise its technological labor skill and reducing the technological material to be used to manufacture the software games and computers. Then, it will have chance to keep the maximum manufacturing level number to software game and computer products as the same time.

CHAPTER THREE

FACILITY MANAGEMENT INFLUENCES AIRPORT AND LOGISTIC EMPLOYEE PERFORMANCE

● **Facility management assists employees reduce maintenance service expenditure**

Facility management provides a variety of non core operations and maintenance services to support any organizations' operation. For logistic organization example, it is possible to provide effective maintenance service to warehouse in order to reduce warehouse facilities to be damaged to bring to spend to buy any new equipment facilities expenditure. So, when the logistic company's warehouse facilities can be maintenance to be the best quality. Then, they can be used these warehouses' machines facilities again. Their performance can assist workers to manufacture any products to keep the most efficiently an raising the best production performance in whole manufacturing process. Then, this logistic company's facility management department can bring to avoid purchase any new machine facilities expenditure spending. One to these warehouses' production machine facilities are kept in the best production performance environment even in long term production need.

I shall indicates airport and warehouse facilities how to influence employees performances as below:

(1) How can comfortable warehouse facilities influence workers' efficiencies in logistic industry ?

The logistic industry's facility management department can create cost savings and efficiency of the warehouse's workplaces. It's machines facilities (production machines) are dealt with the maintenance management of the physical assets maintenance service. FM (facilities management) has been being applied to industrial facilities in logistic and warehouse industry long term as well as maintenance plays a significant role to ensure the full service and the warehousing system, including both building components and equipment in warehouse.

Maintenance service is needed to bring a certain level of availability and reliability of a warehouse facilities system and its components and its ability perform to a standard level of quality. So , it seems that logistic industry's warehouse asset cost reducing. It depends on whether it has one facility management department to provide maintenance service to itself warehouse workplace's production machine facilities and warehouse building itself in order to let workers t feel the manufacturing machines can bring good manufacturing performance to assist them to produce any products in one safe warehouse workplace environment. Hence, the performance measurement of warehouse maintenance issue will be valued to be consider to every warehouse manager and facility manager in logistic industry.

In logistic industry, (FM) works at two level on the one hand, it provides a safe and efficient working environment, which is essential to influence warehouse workers whether how they perform to do their manufacturing tasks or logistic goods delivery tasks in warehouse. When they feel the warehouse is safe environment to work. They will not need to consider anywhere has risk to cause they die by accident in warehouse. Hence, they can concentrate on doing their every tasks . On the other hand, it can involve strategic issues, such as property (warehouse workplace and management, strategy property decision and warehouse facility, e.g. manufacturing machine, facility maintenance and checking planning and maintenance planning development.

However, reducing the operating expense issue will be the main aim when the logistic company feels that it has need to set up one in-house facility management department to carry on any maintenance service for its warehouses' any workplace property and manufacturing machines facilities. So, when the logistic company decides to implement one facility management department, it needs to ensure its facility management department can bring the minimum level of keeping manufacturing performance and efficiency to its warehouses' any manufacturing machines and warehouses' property to avoid to be damaged in short term, such as loss of business due to failure in service, provision of project to customer satisfaction, provision of safe environment, effective utilisation of workplace space, e.g. warehouse effectiveness and communication between the workers and the logistic managers in the warehouse workplace , due to the warehouse's space is not enough maintenance service reliability to the logistic company's warehouse, responsiveness of the warehouse's worker individual negative emotion problem, due to he/she often feels need to work in one unsafe warehouse working environment. Hence, it seems that poor or unsafe warehouse working environment can influence workers feel negative emotion to work to bring low efficiency (inefficiency) or under productive performance in warehouse. It has relationship to influence they to bring psychological negative emotion feeling to work when the organization lacks one effective warehouse management repairing service to be provided to the warehouse's facilities and properties' maintenance needs in order to avoid ineffective measurement and misleading of performance.

Hence, the logistic company's facilities management department often needs to be reviewed whether its maintenance service level is passed to achieve the lowest repair (maintenance) service standard to its warehouse itself property and manufacturing machine or warehouse delivery tool facilities or warehouse lamps' light whether is enough to let workers to see anything clearly to avoid accident occurrence or see anything to work clearly or the warehouse space areas are enough to let they can have enough space to walk or communicate to their team supervisors or deliver any goods more easily in the short distance between the worker's sending goods location and the delivering goods destination in order to avoid because the lacking enough space to cause the accident occurrence , due to the space is not enough to let they deliver their goods to any locations in warehouse.

Hence, it seems logistic company's (FM) department can contribute to the organization's mission, such as avoiding warehouse accident occurrence, inefficiency, not enough and unavailability of the facility for future needs when the warehouse lacks enough space areas to bring poor performance of facility and dangerous warehouse itself property in warehouse, e.g. safe and reliable operations of material handling equipment and maintenance of warehouse facilities, grounds, security system, utilities, plumbing, heating , enough lighting system, air conditioning, warming heater, fire protection, security system alarm etc. facilities in warehouse.

Hence, it seems that if the logistic company expected to reduce to spend lot of excessive manufacturing machine purchase expenditure, lose of workers' life or bring workplace accidents , due to poor warehouse workplace environment, even bringing lawsuit compensation claim loss , due to the worker individual accident or death is caused from the poor warehouse facilities, or bring negative emotion to let the workers feel they are working in unsafe warehouse workplace environment. Then, it ought choose to set up on facility management department in order to provide enough maintenance service to its warehouse to avoid these non essential expenditure causing , due to these poor warehouse facilities factors.

Hence any logistic company ought choose to set up one itself in -house facility management department, it be better than outsourcing its all facilities service to one facility management (maintenance service provider) to help it to deal any kinds of maintenance service in warehouse. Because it is long term maintenance need to its warehouse's any machines and warehouse itself properties. If it chose to find one outsourcing facilitiy management maintenance service provider to replace its in-house facility management department to deal all related facilities maintenance tasks in warehouse. Then, it is possible that it needs to pay long time facilities maintenance service fee to its outsourcing facility management maintenance service provider more than itself facility management maintenance service provision department.

(2) Can facility management influence tourism industry's human resource management influence to improve productivity in airline, travel agent, hotel tourism sectors?

In tourism industry, measuring productivity froma HRM prespective is extremely difficult and has proven to be a limitation within the tourism sector. Due to the customers are not tangible. For example, how can the travel agent measure its travel consultant individual service performance to evaluate whether the travelling customer feels or does not feel satisfactory loyalty from his/her service? How can the airline measure its pilot , airline front-line travelling passenger service attendant indiviual service performance to evaluate whether his/her travelling passenger feels or does not feel satisfactory to whose service performance? Whether airport facility management can influence airline counter service staffs performance ?

However, the complaint number whether it is more or less to the airline or travel agent's service behavior , it does not represent whose service attitude or behavior or performance is poor absolutely because there are many travelling consumers whose complaints are unreasonable , although they feel satisfactory to the airline attendent or airline front -line service staffs individual service performance, but if they feel unhappy to be caused by the airline or travel agent service staff. They will still compain their performance. For this suitation example , it is possible that the travelling passenger is delayed to catch the airplance to fly, due to the country's sudden worse weather influnce, he/she will complain the airline fron-line counter travelling customer service staffs, it concerns when the air plane will arrive the airport, if the airline counter service staff's feedback is that the airplane needs long time arrival. Then, the travelling passengers will complain to the airline counter service staffs in angry. But in fact, the air plane delays to arrive the airport, the airline counter service staffs ought not need responsibilitie to explain the reason why they can not assist the delayed air plane to arrive the country in easier. Furthermore, thy will be complained unreasonably. Hence, it is difficult to measure tourism sector's service staffs ' performance, also the complaint exact number is not one judgement factor to measure their service performance absolutely.

I assume any tourism industry's front -line service airline staffs, they must attempt to serve their travelling passenger in positive service attitude and behavior. So, any tourism industy, how to improve their front -line service staff performance in order to let they to know how to deal unreasonable complaints in sudden unpredictive suitation. Their training materials or contents my include: Teaching them how to provide positive feedback to treat any travelling passenger individual difficult problems or unreasonable complaints in order to reduce their psychological pressure to unknown how to treat these passenger individual related problems when they are facing in airports or travelling agent workplaces. The travelling agent or airline travelling service organizations can attempt to collect measures of employee performance from customers , for example, comment cards in hotel rooms, airplane, travel agent's workplace, mystery shoppers etc. more focus shouls be pleased on this form of evaluation. In order to evaluate the actually place value on the customer ratings to every employee. The all every day, the form of evaluation concerning the actually value on the customer ratings , will be gathered to strategic , it has how many customers feel good or bad ratings to every employee individual performance when every one's tasks are finishing. Due to one month, it can make statistic report to calculate how much performance marks to give to every employee in order to evaluate whether every one's performance is satisfactory to be accepted to the lowest level. If the employee's marks rating is low, his/her department manager can arrange a time and day to meet him/her to discuss whether which aspects of problems who feels in order to give recommendation how to improve his/her service attitude to let customer to give higher marks rating to him/her next time.

Hence tourism industry's service sector organizations need to have one training department to arrange courses how to improve employee service performance in order to let customer to give higher marks rating to very one as well as finding methods how to excite every front line service employee individual loyalty , they can increase their confidence to know how to deal sudden unreasonable complaints in effective and efficient positive attitude. In conclusion, how to improve employee service performance issue will be any tourism service organization's HRM concerning problem. Airports need to arrange how to implement efficient and comfortable and available convenient airport facilities to let any airline service counter staffs feel enjoyable to serve their passengers. They need to know how to find the most effective methods to solve how improvement of front line employee individual performance problem in order to raise the airline or travel agent's quality of service to let itself further customers to feel its service performance is better than others. So, facility management has indirect relationship to influence airport airline service staffs performances.

In conclusion, to decide whether the company ought need or not need facilities maintenance service or either set up in-house facility management department or outsource one facility management maintenance service provider. It depends on whether its organization has how many facilities are used in its workplace, how many staffs are working the workplace, how much size of its workplace, its workplace is office or warehouse or factory, how long time of its facilities' useful time etc. factors , then it can decide whether it needs or does not need one facility maintenance service department or outsourcing facility maintenance service provider to help it to deal any facilities management problem in its organization.

● Facility management role in
organization

When one company feels that it has need facility management service. It can choose to set up either in-house facility management department or seek one outsourcing facility management service provider to help it to arrange any facility management service need. However, this facility management role is only one for the organization. It concerns this question: What facility management maintenance function can bring the benefits to the organization?

It can define that all services required for the management of building and real estate to maintain and increase their value, the means of providing maintenance support, project management and user management during the building life cycle, the integration of multi-disciplinary activities within the built environment and the management of their impact upon people and the workplace. In traditional, (FM) services may include building fabric maintenance, decoration and refurbishment, plant, plumbing and drainage maintenance, air conditioning maintenance, lift and escalator maintenance , fire safety alarm and fire fighting system maintenance, minor project management. All these are hard services. Otherwise, cleaning , security, handyman services, waste disposal, recycling, pes control, grounds maintenance, internal plants. All these are soft services. Additional services, might also include: pace planning, things moving management, business risk assessment, business continuity planning, benchmarking, space management, facilities contract outsourcing service arrangement, information systems, telephony, travel booking facility utility management, meeting room arrangement services, catering services, vehicle fleet management, printing service, postal services, archiving , concierge services, reception services, health and safety advice, environmental management.

All of these services will be every organization's in-house facility soft or hard services needs. So, it explains why some large organizations feel need one effective facility management department to help them to arrange how to implement facility services efficiently in order to achieve cost reducing, raising efficiency and performance improvement aims because one effective facility management control system can influence employee individual productive effort to be raised or reduced indirectly.

However, (FM) can be selected either setting up one in-house (FM) department or outsourcing its services to one facility management service provider to help the organization to solve any kinds of facilities maintain service problems. One on-house (FM) department is a team, it needs employees to deliver all (FM) services. Some specialist services are needed to be outsourced, when the service is on expertise in the company. The no expertise services will be outsourced to simple service contracts, e.g. lift and escalator (FM) department will have direct labour, but it can outsource some specialist to help it to do some complex facilities management service. So, the team leader can of can manage whose team staffs, such as maintenance technicians run low risk operations . Otherwise, the outsourcing facility management service provider needs to help it to operate high risk operations or maintenance vital plant facility management service. Anyway, it can set up in-house (FM) department to arrange specialist direct labour and outsourced (FM) services to more than one facility management service providers to do different kinds of (FM) services. One of these outsourcing (FM) service provider, who can arrange sub-contractors to assist it to finish any (FM) services of it's outsourcing (FM) services are more complex to compare the other sub-contractors (third parties).

● What is a facility manager's role to provide quality service to satisfy its user needs?

We need to know how quality can be defined in facility management and why it should be defined by the customer? How facility managers can find out customer (user) needs? What are the difficulties in finding out users' needs and in delivering quality services? Whether improving quality always means requiring higher cost?

In general, facility manager's major responsibilities may include these major functional areas: longer range and annual facility planning, facility financial forecasting, real estate acquisition and/or disposal, work specification, installation and space management, architectural and engineering planning and design, new construction and/or renovation, maintenance and operations management, maintenance and operation management, telecommunications integration, security and general administrative services. When the facility manager had implemented any one of these FM services for those user. How does he/she provide excellent (FM) service quality ot let whose users to feel satisfactory?

In fact, quality issues can not be considered without customer-oriented perspective service quality involves a comparison of expectation with performance. (FM) service quality is a measure of how well to service level delivered matches customer expectation. So, these issues are (FM) service user's general measurement level requirement. The (FM) manager needs to achieve these the minimum performance measurement level to satisfy whose (FM) user's needs.

However, (FM) service quality has three characteristics: Intangibility, heterogeneity, inseparability. But in fact, (FM) service delivered may be through tangible physical aspects, e.g. factory plant workplace building, machine equipment maintenance, intangible (FM) services, e.g. managing space moving in plant to let staffs to work, managing outsourcing cleaners to clean factory equipment. However, all (FM) service performance often varies, due to the behavior of service personnel. Hence, a well developed job specification and training can help to improve the consistence of services of (FM). Any (FM) production and consumption of many services may are inseparable and they are usually interactions between the (FM) client and the contact person from the service provider.

Hence, it seems that service quality is considered as hard to evaluate. In (FM) service quality, it includes physical quality and interactive non-physical service quality. Physical quality is tangibles: The appearance of the physical facilities, equipment, personnel and communication materials. Non-physical services quality means reliability: The ability to perform the promised service dependably and accurately; responsiveness means the willingness to help customers and provide prompot service to let user to feel; assurance mans the competence of the system in its credibility in providing a courteous and secure service and empathy means the approachability, ease of access and effort taken to understand customers' needs.

Hence, a good performance of (FM) manager , he/she ought satisfy the user's tangible and non-tangible both service quality needs. I recommend that he/she can attempt to predict what are the (FM) customer expects in each (FM) service needs. Then, it can make decision what aspect(s) will be the (FM) users major (FM) service need and what aspect(S) won't be the (FM) users major (FM) service need. Then, he/she can make more accurate decision to arrange time, human resource , cost spending amount arrangement whcther when it ought concentrate on finishing the (FM) major service tasks as well as whether how he/she ought finish the major (FM) service tasks to be more easily, e.g. how to arrange staffs number to finish, how many the minimum staffs number is needed to be arrange the major (FM) service tasks, time arrangement is important factor, because it can influence whether he/she ought finish the major (FM) service tasks today or tomorrow or later in order to have enough time to finish other non-major (FM) service tasks. Instead of time management, staff number arrangement is also important factor , if he/she arranged the excessive staffs number to do the (FM) major services tasks, then it is possible that it will have shortage of staffs number to finish the non-major (FM) service tasks on the day. So, avoiding either major or non-major (FM) services can not finish on the day. The (FM) manager needs to predict when the major (FM) services and the non-major (FM) services which are necessary to be finished in order to have enough time and staffs to assist him/her to finish every day major and non-major (FM) service effectively. Then, the achievement of his/her (FM) major and non-major tangible and non-tangible services , it will have more chance to be performed efficiently by his/her managed staffs.

In conclusion, in any organizations , (FM) manager needs have good predictable effort to evaluate whether when his/her managed team need to finish the major and/or non-major (FM) tasks as well as whether how he/she ought arrange the accurate time and staff number to finish any major and/or non-major (FM) service tasks on the day. Then, his/her leading of (FM) service team can be managed to work more efficiently in order to satisfy her/his (FM) service user's needs.

Facility management how influences
public service transport service performance
● How (FM) space moving management brings employees efficiencies
There are interesting questions: How (FM) can bring value-add to avoid loss or earn more profit to the organization? Can it influence employees to raise performance and improve efficiency ? Some organizations' (FM) service need which is necessary in order to let employees can raise productivity.
It is based on these assumptions: I assume the organizations have completely either outsourced or in-house their (FM) facility management departments will gain more effect on added value than they have no (FM) function as well as organizations have a strong coordination with the (FM) department will gain more added value than organizations with a weak coordination. Organizations in the profit aim can gain more added value than organizations in the not for profit aim sectors.

In fact, any organization is difficult to confirm it has relationship between improving performance, raising efficiency and owning (FM) function in its organization. (FM) could have to do with the attraction of easy but incomplete indicators of efficiency rather than the necessarily and less direct measures if the effectiveness and the relevance of space moving useful management, e.g. whether building has the enough space to let employees to move to work easy in order to raise efficiency, whether the building has excessive furniture and equipment number and they are putted on wrong places to be caused employees move difficulty in the building in order to influence productive performance.

However, how to arrange space moving management to equipment, e.g. copying machines, faxes, productive machines, they are putted on the locations where have enough space to let employees to move to another locations. For example, the building floor has more than 50 employees, but its space is not enough to let these 50 employees to move to any locations to let them to feel easily often. Then, it is possible to cause they feel nervous pressure and they can feel difficult to work , when they are working in a small office space or factory space or warehouse space. Then, the consequence will be under-predictive efficiency or poor performance to any one of these 50 employees in this office or factory or warehouse.

" Facility management is responsible for coordinating all efforts related to planning, designing, and managing buildings and their systems, equipment, and furniture to enhance. The organizations abilty to compete successfully in a rapidly changing world." (F.Becker)

The author explains equipment, workplace internal space designing, furniture space putting location arrangement will have possible to influence employee individual productive performance or efficiency to be raised or reduced in the workplace. Hence, it seems that, in the value chain (FM) belongs to the activity part of the firm. To make the facilities cooperation with each office or factory or warehouse using space moving facility management. Facility space moving management must be linked strategically, tactically and operationally to other support activity to add value to the organization's office or factory or warehouse space moving management arrangement more effectively.

Thus, how to arrangement space moving management issue it will have possible to influence the organization's employee individual productive performance and efficiency in whose workplace. It seems that (FM) space moving management arrangement have indirect relationship to influence the organization's employee individual performance and efficiency , due to they need often to work in the workplace, if they feel moving difficulty , or excessive equipment , furniture number is putting into the small office, factory or warehouse locations, or they feel the office or factory or warehouse has excessive (a lot of) staffs number to work in the small space of office or factory or warehouse. Then, they can not concentrate nervous on finishing every tasks in possible. In long term, their efficiencies will be poor or inefficiencies or their performance won't be improved or causing poor performance in possible.

Instead of the not enough space moving and excessive staffs number factor, it will bring another question: Can enough information systems equipment cause a more efficient and improved performance to the organization staffs in the workplace?

I assume that the office has 100 employees and it has only ten copying machines. So it means that ten employees use one copying machine. Hence, it brings this question: Is it enough to provide only ten copying machines to average ten employees to use? It depends on other factors, e.g. whether any one of these 100 employees needs to print how many documents per day , whether the five copying machines' locations are far away to separate different locations or they are stored in one printing room in the office, whether the day has how many staffs are absent, whether the day has how many printing machine(s) is/ are broken to need to be repaired. Hence, these unpredictable external environment factors will influence whether the five copying machines number is enough to let these 100 employees to use in the office every day. Hence, facility manager ought need to spend to observe average their copying behaviors every day in order to make data record. Many employees need to use copy machines to print documents, average how many document's page number, they need to print, how much average time spending to print their documents, average how many staff absent number on the day. Even, if the all five copying machines are stored in the printing room, calculating the staffs number whether how many staffs need more than five minutes to walk to the printing room to print their documents many staffs need to spend five minute to walk to the printing room, and they have other urgent tasks to wait to finish. It is possible to influence their efficiency, due to they often need to spend more than five minutes to walk to the printing room to print documents. If there are many staffs need to often to print documents, but their printing task will have many time, e.g. 20 separate printing tasks. Then, they need to spend at least

(20x5) 100 minutes to spend time to walk to the printing room to print their documents. It must influence that they should not finish the other urgent tasks on the day. If there are many staffs to spend much time to walk to the printing room in the least 20 separate printing time or more on that day. All the facility manager needs to evaluate whether all the five copy machines are stored in the printing room whether it is the best location decision or they ought need be separated to put on different office locations in their workplaces, even he/she ought need to evaluate whether it is enough copying machines number, when the office has only 5 copying machines. He/she ought need to buy more copying machines number to satisfy any one of these 100 employee individual copying task need.

In conclusion, effective office or factory or warehouse space moving facility management will be one part task of (FM) function. If the office or factory or warehouse can have accurate equipment, machine , furniture number to avoid excessive or shortage number problem to cause employees often feel moving difficult problem in their workplace when they need to move to another location to work in office or warehouse or factory as well as whether the staff needs often spend time to wait the another employee to use the copying machine to print whose document or fax machine to deliver whose document. Then, it is not that fax or printing machines number is not enough to provide the employees to use in the office or warehouse or factory workplace.

Hence, (FM) includes space moving facility management to equipment , machines, furniture number as well as choosing anywhere is(are) the suitable location (s) arrangement to putting or storing these facilities in workplace as well as decision of the staff number and the workplace area size whether it has excessive staffs number to cause these staffs need to work in the small area size of office or warehouse or factory workplace. So, the organization ought need to decide whether it needs to reduce the office's staffs number to let them to work in another more suitable locations in another workplace. Hence, all these facilities space moving management and staffs and workplace size issues will be (FM) manager's consideration issues, because these external environment factors will influence employee individual efficiency and performance to be poor to cause low valued to its organization in long term in possible .

● Predictive the choosing right
data asset and (FM) analytics

solutions to boost public

transportation service quality

Can gather the choosing right data public transportation service station facilities asset and analytics, it can give recommendation to help any organization to boost service quality? (FM) analytics data can be applied to public transportation service industry to be supported how and why the train, train, ferry , ship, air plane, underground train public transportation tools' time arrival and leaving information notice board and automated ticket paying machines facilities are putting on or stored any where locations in order to boost passengers to feel their facilities locations are convenient to let them to buy tickets and see the arrival and leaving time for the next public transportation tool from the information notice electronic board machine. So, it seems that these public transportation tools' station facilities locations can influence passengers to feel the public transportation service company how to consider to its passenger's buying ticket needs and next public transportation tool's arrival and leaving time information needs in order to boost its passengers use service quality and let them to feel better service reliable performance in any train, tram, ferry , ship, underground tram, airplane stations.

As these public transportation service organizations need to learn data analytics represent an opportunity for its ticket paying machine equipment facilities as well as the next transportation tool arrival and leaving time information notice board electronic equipment facilities anywhere the locations are the most suitable to put on or store these equipment to let passengers to walk to the ticket paying machines to buy the ticket to catch the train, tram, underground train, ferry, airplane, taxi, ship more easily. So, they do not need to spend more time to find these facilities locations and spend more time to queue to wait to buy ticket to catch the public transportation tool in stations conveniently. Instead of where is the seeking ticket paying machine location, where is the next public transportation tool arrival and leaving information notice time , these both issues will be any public transportation tool's passenger's main needs.

Hence, how to spend time to seek where the next public transportation tool's arrival and leaving time information electronic notice machine location and where the ticket paying machine location , these both factors will influence any passengers' positive or negative emotion causing. For example, if the passenger feels difficult to find the ticket paying machine in the large area size train station or /and he/she feels difficult to find the train time arrival and leaving information to let him/her to know when the next train will arrive the station. Due to he/she feels difficult to find the train ticket paying machine, he/she needs to spend much time to find any one ticket paying machine in the train station. Then, it will influence him/her to choose another public transportation tool to replace the train public transportation tool, e.g. he/she can choose to catch tram, underground train, taxi, bus, ferry, taxi, ship to replace train. So, it seems ticket paying machine and time arrival and leaving information notice electronic equipment 's location putting or stored choice will be one factor to influence the passenger to choose another kind of public transportation tool to replace train at the moment. When, he/she feels that he/she arrives the destination in the most short time. Then, the public transportation service organization (FM) manager has responsibility to evaluate whether there are enough ticket paying machines number to let passengers do not need to spend more time to queue to buy tickets to catch the public transportation tool in short time as well as there are enough time arrival and leaving for next transportation tool to let passengers to know. It will be their concerning issues when they arrive the public transportation service tool's station.

Hence, predictive passenger individual walking behavior can help the public transportation service organization to choose whether where are the most convenient and attractive locations to let the ticket paying machines and the arrival and leaving time information electronic board machines to be putted on or stored in the suitable station positions in order to let many passengers can find these essential facilities in stations very easily. So, gathering data concerns passenger walking behavior in the public transportation service any stations, which can help the facility manager to make more accurate evaluation to attempt to predict whether where the locations are common places to let passengers to choose to walk daily or where the locations are not common places to let passenger to choose not to walk daily in general. Then, he/she can apply these data of different locations in the stations to evaluate whether anywhere they will have many passengers to choose to walk or whether anywhere they won't have many passengers to choose to walk in order to make more accurate decision whether anywhere are the most suitable locations to let the ticket paying machines and the time arrival and leaving information electronic board equipment to be putter on or stored in order to let them to feel it is so easier to let them to find.

Anyway, calculating each station's passenger number per day issue is important to predict whether where , there are many passengers choose to walk or where, there are not many passengers choose to walk in these different public transportation service stations in order to evaluate whether where the stations' different ought put on paying ticket machines or time arrival and leaving information electronic boards in order to let they feel very easy to buy tickets and seeing the next arrival and leaving time information for the kind of public transportation service tool conveniently in the different stations. Moreover, if the station has no enough ticket paying machines number to be supplied to let passengers need to spend more than ten minute time to wait to buy ticket to catch the kind of public transportation service tool in every queue every day. Then it will cause them to choose another kind of public transportation tool to catch go to working place or entertainment place to replace it to on that day. Then, it will cause these passengers who often do not like to queue in the kind of public transportation service tool's any stations, who will not choose to go to anywhere of this kind of public transportation service tool's any stations again. Hence, in long term this kind of public transportation service tool will lose many passengers. Thus, calculating each station's busy time of passengers number , which can predict when it is the busy time and it can make more accurate decision whether the station has need to increase enough ticket paying machines number in order to bring enough supply number to satisfy passengers' ticket purchase need in the busy time.

In conclusion, gathering above all stations' public transportation service equipment facilities number, storing positions data and every station's passenger walking behavior data, they are necessary to any public transportation tool service industry, because these equipment number and storing locations will influence them to make decisions to choose another kind of public transportation tool to replace it's transportation service if they often feel difficult to find these facilities in its different stations. Thus, it is part of task to facility manager's responsibility if the public transportation service organization expects it won't lose many passengers , due to these external environment factor influence and it also implies cheap ticket price does not guarantee the passengers will choose to catch this kind of public transportation service tool to go to anywhere.

- The relationship between facility
management and productive
efficiency

It is one interesting question: Can facility management function bring benefits to raise productive efficiency to organizations? I shall indicate some cases to attempt to explain this possible occurrence chance as below:

● Facility management benefit to office workplace

In private organizations, when the firm has facility management department, whether it can bring efficient administration to influence clerks to work efficiently in office, e.g. reducing administrative time or shorten time to work in administrative processes, in order to achieve minimizing clerk number labor cost. How to design office facilities to let office staffs to feel comfortable to work and reducing their pressure to work. It seems that office working environment will influence office staff individual performance. If the office working environment could improve efficiency and creativity of services to satisfy office workers' comfortable working environment needs. It will reduce every administration manager's working pressure when he/she needs often to find methods to attempt to encourage whose administrative clerks to avoid to waste working time to do some non-major administration tasks.

Hence, how to design or allocate or arrange office any facilities' stored locations or whether how many equipment number is the enough to store in the locations, which will influence office employees' working attitude in order to raise or reduce their administration tasks efficiency indirectly, e.g. the office is clean or dirty, whether office reception has enough information telephone switchboard operation facilities, whether every clerk's table has enough computers number to supply to every to use, whether internet speed is fast or slow in order to let any employees can send and receive email to communicate or download any document from internet in short time, whether data processing and computer system maintenance service supply is enough to be repaired to employees' computers immediately when their computers are broken to wait repair, whether website editing facilities operation whether is enough to link to office every staffs in order to let any office staffs can apply internet to do their tasks conveniently in short time. Hence, all of these general office equipment facilities whether they are enough supplied and their stored positions anywhere are the suitable to assist any clerks to work conveniently, they will influence every office employee's administrative and productive efficiency indirectly as well as all faxes, copying machines, computers, whether internet linking maintenance service time is short or long to prepare to any office employees to use conveniently any time, these different issues will also influence every employee individual efficiency in office. Hence, it concludes that office working environment, facilities supply number, facilities maintenance service and facilities location storing both factors will influence employee individual administrative productive efficiency in office.

● facility management benefits to service working environment

Can effective facility management improve service working environment to raise employee individual work performance? It is a concern about the quality of service to its customer question. The term" standards and goals" are often used to measure staff individual service performance whether he/she can serve to customers to let them to feel this staff's service performance or attitude is good or bad.

Is the service workplace working environment facilities enough, it will influence customer service staff individual performance.

For shopping center service industry case example, for this situation, e.g. shopping center's facilities are enough or are placed to the suitable locations in order to let the shopping center's customers to feel comfortable to shopping when they enter this shopping center as well as whether the shopping center's facilities can influence the customer service staffs to serve whose shopping customers easily or difficult, due to whether the shopping center's facilities whether are adequate supplied or their locations are the best suitable positions to influence their service performance to let them to feel easier or comfortable to serve their customers in any large size shopping centers. For example, whether the lamps' lighting energy is enough to let the shoppers to feel safe to walk to visit any shops when there are many shoppers were walking to cause crowd and they feel difficult to walk to avoid any body contact to any one in busy time when the shopping center has no enough lights to let them to see anywhere in the shopping center's dark environment. Then it will influence customer service staffs to feel difficult to find any shopping center customers, e.g. when two shopping center customers are fighting in one location where is far away to the shopping customer service staffs and securities in the shopping center, because the shopping center is large and it has no enough light to let the customer service staffs and securities to find their frighting location to deal their fighting behavior and other shopping center's shoppers will feel very dangerous to walk their fighting location to avoid to close them. Then, it will has possible to cause death or hurt to any one of these two fighting shoppers ,even other shoppers' life. Because the shopping center's securities and customer service staffs who need to spend much time to find their fighting location, it will delay they can bring the policemen to their fighting location when they arrive this shopping center's destination in short time in order to solve their fighting behavior to influence all shoppers' life in this shopping center. Hence, the shopping center whether it has enough lamps number and the lamps' light whether is enough, these lighting facilities will influence any shopping center customer service staffs and securities who can spend less time to arrive any locations to deal any urgent matters.

For another situation in shopping center, if the shopping center has no enough paying telephone service facilities to supply shoppers to phone to anyone when they feel need to phone to any in the shopping center. Then, it will lead to some shoppers decide to find where the shopping center's reception's telephone to supply to them to phone call to anyone. If they are ten shoppers are waiting to use the shopping center's reception telephone to phone call to their friend or family within one minute. Thus, it will influence the reception customer service staffs feel difficult to arrange how to distribute the only one telephone to these ten shoppers to use to phone call their friend or family when they are queuing within their one minute waiting time in the shopping center's reception. If these ten shoppers can not use the reception telephone to phone call anyone. hen, they will feel dissatisfactory and complain to the reception service staffs politely. So, lacking enough facilities in the shopping center's any where, it will possible to influence their shopping centers' shoppers to feel all shopping center's service staff individual performance to be poor. It means that if the shopping center expects to improve customer satisfaction to its customer service staff's behavioral performance, it meets have enough facilities to be supplied in the shopping center to let its shoppers to feel it is one comfortable and safe shopping center. In conclusion, shopping center's facilities will have possible to influence shoppers' feeling to evaluate its customer service staffs to evaluate whether their service attitudes are good or poor indirectly.

● Can facility management improve productivity

The productivity means resources (input) is therefore the amount of products or services (output), which is produced by them. Hence, higher (improved) productivity means that more is produced with the same expectation of resource, i.e. at the same cost is terms of land materials, machine, time or labor. Alternatively, it means same amount is produced at less labor cost in term of land, material, machine, time for labor that is utilized. So, it brings this question: How can facility management improve productivity? I shall explain as these several aspects, it is possible to be improved productivity from (FM) successfully.

Improved productivity of farm land: If the farming land has better facility management to bring advantages by using better seed, better facilities of cultivation and most fertilizer. It is in the agricultural sense is increased (improved). So, facility management can bring benefits to any land resource to raise productivity in possible. It implies that the productivity of land used for better facility management of industrial purposes is said to have been increased if the output of products or service within that area of industrial land is increased output aim.

Improved productivity of material: If the factory has improved better equipment by facility management method to assist skillful workers to raise the manufacture cloth number, then the productivity of the cloth number is improved by (FM) method.

Improved productivity of labour: When the factory has good manufacturing equipment facilities to be supplied to improve methods of work to product more producing number per hour, then (FM) improved productivity of worker. Hence, in any workplaces, when organization has good facilities, it will influence employees to raise productivities in possible, because they need often to improved equipment facilities manufacture products to achieve higher production number aim.

● Can facility management raise bank employee
productivity

Bank workplace environment is busy, the bank counter service staffs need to contact many bank clients to help them to serve or withdraw money from bank's counters. Whether does the quality of environment in bank workplace will influence the determination level of employee's motivation, subsequent performance productivity in bank working environment. For example, if the bank's staffs need work under inconvenient conditions , it will bring low performance and face occupational health diseases causing high absenteeism and turnover.

In general, bank size is usually small, it will have many bank clients enter bank to contact counter staffs to need them to help them to save or withdraw money. So, it will bring air pollution the crowd queue in every bank counter challenge when the bank has many people are queue waiting in counters to queue. So, bank working condition problem relates to environmental and physical factors which will influence every bank counter staff individual working performance to serve bank clients satisfactory. However, bank staffs need to deal many documents concern every client personal data every day. So, they need to spend much time to use computer and painting machines. This is particularly true for these employees who spend most of the day operating a computer terminal in bank workplace. As more and more computers are being installed in workplaces, an increasing number of business has been adopting designs for bank offices installment. So, bank needs have effective facilities management design because of demand of bank staffs for more human comfort.

An good equipment facility management for bank staffs to use conveniently, it is assumed that better workplace environment can motives bank employees and produces better productivity. Hence, bank office environment can be described in terms of physical and behavioral components to influence bank staffs to work inefficiently. To achieve high level of bank employee productivity, bank organizations must ensure that the physical environment in conductive to bank different department organizational needs, facilitating interaction and privacy, formality and informality, functional and disciplinarily, e.g. house loan or private loan departments, counter service department, visa card application department.

Thus, in a high safe privacy facility management working environment will let different department bank staffs feel safe to worry about privacy loss in possible. So, the improving bank facility to bring safe and high privacy to avoid bank client individual loss in working environment issue, the facility management can be results to bring these benefits, such as in a reduction in a number of complaints and absenteeism and an increase in productivity.

● Can (FM) create value to organization?

(FM) can reduce managing facilities as a strategic resource to add value to the organization and its overall performance, e.g. saving the energy in building and take care of shuttle buses and parking facilities space management for , on economic efficiency and effectiveness, or good price and value for the organization.

If the organization expects to apply (FM) process to save energy, it depends on possible input factors, i.e. interventions in the accommodation facilities services. So, it seems that the organization expects to save its energy consumption in its building. It needs have good space management facilities between parking its shuttle buses in its property's car park.

Why does space facility management is important to influence efficiency and productivity. For one school's building example, when the school decides none of the two gymnasiums student sport entertainment centers to be built in order to reduce financial cost and higher benefits. Remarkably, the use of space with the school overall strategic goals , such as creating spaces that better can support the teaching, motivate students and teachers, attract more students and increase the utilisation of existing space to accommodate an increasing number of students.

If it hopes to make high quality teaching facilities on student's choice where to study. The school will need to choose to build either one comfortable and new design facility teaching accommodation or build two gymnasium sport entertainment centers in its limited land space either for students' learning or sport aim. Due to it feels new teaching accommodation can make more attractive to increase students numbers to choose it to study more than building two new gym sport centers to let them do sport in school.

Hence, space choice (FC) management strategy will be one important considerable issue, when the organization has limited land space resources to make choose to build any constructions in order to increase many clients number. Such as the school organization has limited storage land resource to let it to build either two gymnasium sport entertainment centers or one new teaching accommodation in order to attract many students to choose it to learn. Hence, it needs to gather data to make more accurate evaluation to decide how to apply its space facility to choose to build these both kinds of buildings in order to achieve the attractive student learning choice aim, so whether the two sport entertainment activity centers or one new teaching accommodation choice, it needs to gather information to decide whether the school ought to choose to build which kind of building in order to achieve the increase of student number aim, so space facility management will be this school's land shortage problem.

● The relationship between facility
management and consumer
behavior

How and why shop facility management can influence consumer individual shopping behavior? If it is possible, what shop facility management factors can influence their consumption decision when they enter the shop to plan to buy anything. I shall indicate some shop case studied to explain whether how and why every shop's facility management can influence consumer individual consumption desire when any one consumer enters any shops.

● Shop's low ceiling height location (FM) influence consumer behavior

Can the shop's ceiling height influence shoppers' shopping behavior? Can the shop's variation in ceiling height can influence how consumers process information to decide to make purchase decision in the shops, e.g. for this situation, when the consumer enters the shop, he/she feels the ceiling height is low and it has a lamp will contact his/her head in possible. So, he/she chooses to move far away from the low ceiling location in the shop. It is possible that shop's ceiling low height and the lamp locates at the ceiling low height position will influence many customers' choices to leave the low ceiling height and lamp location, then the shop's low ceiling height will have possible to influenced many customers to choose to find the another shop to buy the similar kind of products , due to the lamp locates in the low ceiling height, so this lamp and low ceiling height will be possible factor to influence any shoppers who won't choose to walk to this dangerous location in the shop. If the shop's all spaces are ceiling height and it has many lamps are located at the low ceiling height spaces. Then, it will be serious to cause many shoppers do not want to spend too much time to choose any products in the shop because they feel dangerous to walk to the any low ceiling height lamps' locations in the shop.

Hence, hoe to design the different concept may be activated by the showroom ceiling if it were relatively high, as it tends to be in mall stores, versus low, as it is in most strip mall shops and outlet centers. Relatively high ceilings may bring safe shopping emotion to let any consumers to feel thoughts related to freedom, whereas lower ceilings may let consumers to feel dangerous to walk the locations in any shops. Hence it seems any shops ought not neglect whether their ceiling height is tall and the lamps ought avoid to locate in any low ceiling height locations in order to influence consumers number to be decreased.

● Can house facility management influence consumer individual purchase intention?

When one new property is built, whether the property consumers will consider how the new property is facility to influence their purchase intention to the property will the new property's (FM) influence buyers in real estate markets' preferences choice and living interest. Any new property's internal characteristics of the house unit itself , such as rooms available, when example, of external are location, accessibility to utilities services and facilities will have possible to influence the property buyer's final property purchase decision, so it seems that even the property price is cheap, it is not represent the property buyer will choose to buy the property, if he/she feels the property's facility management is poorer to compare other similar kinds of properties.

So, it can help real estate analysts better explain and predict the behavior of decision makers in real estate markets. Property consumers will search for property information, concerns the property's quality, price distinctiveness, ability, facility management, service of the property's external environment to decide whether the property is high value to choose to buy to compare other kinds of properties.

However, the external environmental forces, such as limited resources, e.g. time or financial will influence whose property consumption choice and living the property's satisfaction feeling (represent) a feedback from post-property purchase reflection used to inform subsequent decisions. The process of the property buyer's leaving experience will serve to influence the extent to which the property consumer how to consider future next time property purchases decision and new information methods. Hence, when one property consumer chooses to buy a house, it refers house features are house internal attributes , such as quality of building, the design as well as internal and external design, which are important factors for a property consumer when he/she needs to select and purchases one house.

The other (FM) factors which can influence the property consumers' needs, include living space as features, such as the size of kitchen, bathroom, bedroom, living bath and other rooms available in the house. The environment of housing area is also important factor, e.g. the condition of the hood, attractiveness of the area, quality of houses, type of houses, type of houses, density of housing, wooded area or free coverage, slope of the attractive views, open space, non-residential uses in the areas vacant sites, traffic noise, level of owner-occupation in , level of education in level of income in, security from crime, quality of schools, religious of , transportation , shopping center, sport entertainment can be supplied to close to the house area. All these human related issue of the property's location will also influence the property buyer's living location selection. Hence, above (FM) influence property consumer purchase behavior, it is based on the relationship behavior. The consumer's house purchase intention and house features, living space, environment and distance to recreation center, supermarket, library etc. public facilities variable (FM) factors.

In conclusion, the house internal space facility management and external environment facility management factors will influence property consumer individual house purchase intention.

● The effects of in-store shelf design facility management factor influences consumer behavior

Can every store retailer's shelf design influence supermarket and large retail stores shoppers' behaviors when they visit the stores? However, currently many stores tend to build on traditional and repetitive design for their store shelf layout, it brings results in outdated store layouts.

Another important store shelf layout design aspect, retailer should consider carefully is the allocation of products on shelves. So, it seems that efficient shelf space allocation management does not only minimize the economic threats of empty product shelves, it can also lead to higher consumer satisfaction, a better customer relationship.

Why does supermarket shelves design is important? Any retail tore will sell product category within a shelf. They can use the same nominal category , e.g. crisps next to light crisps, same food product shelf. Anyway, a goal-based shelf display can contain several product, that determine a common consumer goal, e.g. fair trade. Hence, these two categorical product structuring methods are also described in terms of how to put product, or food on shelf benefit and attribute -based product categories.

These shelf design food or product storing method will have more influence consumers to choose to buy the supermarket or retail store food or products more easily , due to products, or food put on their shelf very convenient and systematic to attract consumers' shopping consideration to the supermarket or retail store.

● Music (FM) environment influence consumer consumption desire

Is it possible that shop music (FM) environment can raise consumer purchase desire? In one shop or supermarket, it can provide soft music (FM) equipment to let consumers can listen soft music or songs in the supermarket or retail shop when the are staying to spend more time shopping and whether soft music facility can be expected to raise customer individual value-added options to the music facility shop in the supermarket or retail shop.

Can the music facilities prolong consumers to stay in the store? It is possible that tempo soft music can influence consumers to stay longer time in restaurants and supermarkets and retail shops. It is possible that the different types of music (FM) in any supermarket, restaurant, retail shop owning music listening facility shopping environment. It will have possible to influence consumers to prolong staying in their shops. For example, one wine selling retail shop has classical music (FM) listening equipment to let consumers to listen when they enter the wine shop, it is possible to cause consumers to choose to buy more expensive wine products. Some researchers indicate when the wine shop owns classical music facility to let all consumers can list classical music when they walk in the wine ship, it can evoke the wine consumers to choose to buy purchasing higher prices wine products in the long term classical music listening environment. Otherwise, in a fitness sport center, musical fir and excite or popular music (FM) environment can attract fitness sport players' emotion to play and kind of fitness sport facility longer time. Also, in one supermarket, the soft music facilities listening environment can persuade or attract food consumers to spend more time in the mall consuming food or beverage also purchase other products more easily, due to they will listen soft music to be influenced to choose to prolong staying time in the supermarket. It seems that it has relationship between retail shop's music facility environment and consumer's emotion will be influenced by these different kinds of soft music or songs to raise consumption desire in the supermarket, if some consumers like to prolong to stay longer consuming time in the owning music facility environment's retail shop.

In fact, some researchers indicate the owning background music facility selling environment's ship , it can affect consumer decision making, memory, concentration consumption desire. So, classical , jazz soft music facility ought be installed in restaurants, retail shops, restaurants' environment. Otherwise, popular , exciting, noise, pop music facility ought be installed in fitness sport centers, theme park entertainment parks business places in order to influence fitness sport players or theme park entertainers to prolong playing or entertaining time to feel real sport or entertainment theme park playing machine facility's entertainment enjoyable feeling as well as attracting restaurant or supermarket or retail shop's consumers to prolong their staying time to make consumption decisions. Hence, it seems that music facility environment can raise consumers' consumption desire in possible.

● University bookstore atmospheric factors how to influence student's purchase book behavior?

Any university bookstore how to do international control and structuring of book internal environment to raise students' purchase book desires in university itself school's bookstore, it will be one popular question to any universities. Hence, whether the university bookstore internal (FM) factors include: lighting, music, colors, scents, temperature, layout and general cleanliness as well as university external factors include: the university bookstore shape/size, windows, university parking facility for students availability and location, which can play an influential role of the university bookstore image in order to influence the university itself students to choose to buy books from themselves bookstore or university outside bookstores.

Whether the university student needs to spend how long individual learning time and how much learning nervous to spend time to choose any kinds of book in the universiity bookstore or outside bookstores, this issue , he/she will consider. Because he/she does want to expect spend much time and nervous to choose to buy books in any bookstore. If the university's bookstore physical location and internal (FM) image can let its target student customers to feel it's all book products are stored in any attractive internal book shelves places, e.g. the cheapest and the most expensive different subjects of text books are stored in one system method to bring the positive image of value and quality in order to let university target student customers can find their books' choice location to spend less time to search any books to read in the unviersiity bookstore easily.

However, due to learning time is shortage to every university student of the university's book shelves can display all text books in the attractive right locations in the university bookstore as well as the university's bookstore ought has an adequate space to let university students to walk to anywhere and find any subjects of text books and compare their book sale prices in the bookstore's any shelves' locations easily when they walk to the subject of book shelf location, then they can make accurate decision either to buy the right kind of subject book or not buy it to read in the short time. They will feel their book choice purchase decision making process won't influence their learning time in themselves universiity. Then, the university students will be influenced by themselves university's bookstore's attractive external university facilities in the university's any teaching places and the university's bookstore internal attractive environment facility image which can influence the students to make final choices to buy their liking books to read from their university's itself bookstore. Hence, the university's bookstore internal and external building environment (FM) design factors will influence its students whether choose to buy from themselves bookstore or another outside general bookstore.

● How and why does retail atmospheric environment influence consumers behavior in retail shop?

Any shop's internal facility management design can influence atmospheric environment to influence consumer individual shopping desire, e.g. colour, lighting, music, crowding, design and layout factors, which internal shop (FM) environment can influence the first time shopping visiting client ' cognitive process how to feel the shop store image. Such as if the store's (FM) environment can bring enjoyable and fun and happy image to let them to feel shopping's enjoyment.

In conclusion, when consumers will like to stay longer time in the store. Due to the store's internal (FM) atmospheric environment can attract them to stay longer time in the store. Then, the customer's shopping value will raise and it can bring purchasing intention and shopping satisfaction. How can (FM) influence retail atmospheric physical (FM) environment ? Can (FM) bring indirect relationship to influence how the consumer individual causes positive or negative purchase intention when he/she has influence to prolong staying desire in the store, when the shop has good (FM) , it will bring long time to make consumption chance in the shop.

● Facility management influences
consumer satisfactory service
level

Can facility management (FM) quality influence consumer satisfactory service feeling? Any organization's facility management can improve the effectiveness of the maintenance organization. It can provide improved operational and maintenance functions to maintain the physical environment to support the overall mission. However, any organization will consider whether it improves its facilities, it will raise consumer satisfactory feeling when it provides the service to them, e.g. education service industry, when students need to often to attend any school's classrooms or lecture halls, computer rooms, libraries, all these facilities will be student's learning environment. If these school facilities can be maintenance to let students to feel comfortable to enjoy to study in their schools' any learning locations. Then, it has possible that to bring their enjoyable learning feeling in theirs schools.

● How school's facility management influences student's learning satisfactory feeling.

However, in education industry case, the school's facility management has those criteria can be used to measure effectiveness. Student individual response time between the student's request for computer use service in school computer rooms, library reading service in school library , classroom computer facilities and tables, chairs etc. furniture supplies service and the facility management supply number and available to useful time. If the student believes that the response time is too long when he/she feels need to use any school facilities, the actual number of seconds or minutes, he/she needs to wait how long time to queue to use his/her school's any facilities in library, classroom, computer room. So, the student's queue waiting time to use any his/her school's facilities, it can measure the school's facility management effectiveness.

● Scheduling of preventive maintenance activities.

It schedules of any maintenance activities are not arranged effectively to the school. Then, it will influence students' poor learning facility service to their school. For their situation, when the school's first floor has two men toilets are damaged. They are needed to be required. However, it is one week period, the first floor 100 students can not use the first floor men toilets. Hence, in this week, all 100 students need to go to other floors toilets to often use. They will feel busy and time is not enough when they need to attend to any classrooms to listen the first floor classrooms teachers' lesson. If he/she arrives the first floor classroom too late, due to he/she needs to go to another floor male toilets to queue to use. Then, he/she will feel angry and worries about whose absent or late attending classroom behavior when the lesson's teacher has attended early in the first floor classroom , and he teacher will need him/her to explain why he/she will go to this classroom lately, if his/her explanation won't be accepted to attend to the first floor classroom too late in the week. So, arrangement maintenance schedule to any school's facilities issue is importnt to influence student's satisfactory feeling to the school. Also, lacking of preventive maintenance activities will bring results in unscheduled shutdown of critical equipment can have an unrecoverable impact on the school's good learning environment providing to student's mission.

In fact, however in any organizations, such as school, ship, office etc. organizations, achieving balance of effectiveness and efficient difficulties and takes time and effort on the part of management and staff. It is not enough to establish an optimal relationship between these two parts. It has another factor that organizations need to consider costs. In today's budget tightening environment, decreasing expenses requires accepting a lower level of efficiency and effectiveness. The goal is to determine the point at which decreasing efficiency and effectiveness is no longer acceptable before that point is reached.

It brings this question : How to apply facility management knowledge to rise efficiency and effectiveness in order to improve quality standard of service to satisfy consumers' needs in short time? Such as school's facilities service case. What factors can influence student's level of satisfaction with regards to higher educational facilities services? It seems that any school's facilities will influence its students how to satisfy its education service indirectly. Because they need often to go to school to learn. So, any school's facilities, e.g. classrooms, computer rooms, libraries, toilets, lecture halls, canteens, sport and entertainment centers, research laboratories, school car parks, student enquiry counters, all these places to the school's any students will attend. So, how raise schools' facilities improvement to satisfy students' learning needs in the school's any locations which will have help to influence it student individual satisfaction level to the school's service, instead of every teacher individual teaching performance service to the school's students.

For any service organizations , such as hotels, restaurant, financial institutions, retail stores and hospitals etc. The physical environment can influence how customers' evaluation of their service. Due to service has intangible nature, so customers will rely on evaluate service quality.

Any higher education institutions are education service providing organizations. They need have comfortable and enjoyable educational environment to be provided to the students to attend the school's any places in order to meet whose learning expectations and studying experience needs. So, the school's facility management will be one factor to influence student's learning satisfaction when they expect to attend the school's any locations or places to let them to feel the school's learning environment have good facility management feeling.

In fact, if the school has comfortable classrooms or lecture halls educational environment to let its students to feel, it will bring assistance to raise their learning satisfactory feeling. So, comfortable learning facility management environment is one kind of school's facility service characteristics, it includes intangibility, perishability, inseparability and variability. So, they are every student individual learning feeling when they are attending to the school's any learning locations. So, school's facility management service feeling will influence whether they expect to choose this school to study. If the school's facility management learning environment is more comfortable and teaching facilities are better to compare other schools' facilities. Then, it will have possible to attract many students to choose this school to study. Such as any educational organizations, instead of the teachers (lecturers and professors) whose educational level is influence students number. The university's building environment will influence students' learning feeling, when they attend in the university. The facilities include laboratories, lecture theatres an offices, but also residential accommodations, catering facilities, sports and recreations centers because university students need have university life feeling to let them to fell the university can give welfare services , e.g. medical services, career guidance, sport entertainment, residential accommodation etc. service, instead of educational learning service in classrooms and lecture theatres. Hence, university's diversification facilities services are needed to satisfy university students to choose it to study, instead of university teacher's educational performance. When one student can enroll the university to study from secondary education institution. The admitted student will usually consider two aspects to decide to choose the university to study. One aspect is the academic programs, of sequence of courses choices and the another aspect is the university's facilities whether they can satisfy their university life need, e.g. library, dorms, bookstore, food canteen , gym's sport entertainment, education technological facilities in the classrooms and lecture theatres to let the students to feel the university's teaching facilities are achieved his/her learning demand.

So, these two factors (teaching and learning and facilities) are linked to each other to influence student's total school learning experience and attitude towards a particular institution and this is termed as value chain in the student's learning process in the university. Hence, student individual evaluation variables will include teaching staff, teaching method, enrolment and facility enough supply actual service need.

However, the university's facilities, such as any residential accommodation, canteen, library , classroom, lecture theatre, sport gym, entertainment center will be their useful facilities need to satisfy their learning, entertainment and eating ,even living need in residential accommodation in the school's learning life experience every day. If one student chooses to live in the university residential accommodation . All of his/her learning and eating and living time and spending will be calculated to the university's any facilities to let him/her to feel it can provide enough facilities to let him/her to enjoy.

Hence, the facility management factor, such as overall campus environment, library, laboratory, classroom, lecturer theatre size and facility supply of on campus accommodation, welfare right service, parking areas, cafeteria , sport center etc. They will be every students facilities service needs from the university supplies choice. So, any university ought not neglect how to improve itself university's space area facilities to achieve satisfy their needs after they choose this university to study. Hence, any university's facility management will influence how the student's satisfactory learning service feeling when he/she chooses the university to study.

In conclusion, better facility management will attract more students to choose the university to study. Otherwise, worse facility management will not attract more students to choose to study the school. Hence, it seems that the school's facility management factor has relationship to influence student's satisfactory feeling, instead of teacher individual teaching performance factor to the school.

● Property facility management influences householder buying behavior

One new property's low price is attractive factor to influence property buyer individual preference choice. Does the new individual's facility management factor influence the property buyer's preference choice decision, if the property buyer feels its facility management is better than other similar properties, even it's price is higher than other properties. I shall indicate some cases to analyze this possibility as below:

Some properties' facility management service quality has possible to create true value for any property buyers when they consider the calculation ingredients to make decision whether to new property has higher value to choose to buy. The factors may include: price, natural environment, transportation tools convenient available, shopping centers supplies, the neighour quality, and the property's internal facility management etc. factors.

In fact, car or house purchase buyers, they have similar behaviors. It is that car's buyers will consider the car's machines whether they are safe to drive on roads, instead price, manufacture loyalty factors. It is possible that the car's machines quality factor will be preference to any car buyers when they make preference decisions to choose which brand its cars are the suitable. However, if the car's brand is famous and its appearance beautiful and price is cheap. But the car consumer feels its machine qualities are unsafe to let the driver to drive on road. Then, the car's poor machine quality factor will influence the car buyer's decisions to choose to buy this car. It can influence the car buyer individual car purchase decision.

The car buyer's behavior is similar to property buyer's behavior. Although, the new property price is cheap, good neigh ours are living near to the new property's location, shopping centers and transportation tools are available to near to this new property's area. But if the property buyers' feels its facility management is poor quality to compare other similar properties. Then, the poor quality of facility management factor will have possible to influence the property buyers whose final buying decision to choose to buy this new property. It brings this question: How and why can the facility management poor quality factor influence property consumers' preference choice?

In general, all property consumers won't know whether the new property's facility management is good or bad quality , they need to spend time to visit to the new property in order to observe whether its internal facility is satisfactory to his/her acceptable level. In simple, their purchase decision will regard to how to allocate household budget, how the household's economic resources are influenced, e.g. for travelling, visits to restaurants, comparing the different similar types of property product groups, e.g. apartments or houses or houses of a givn size data. For example, if one property's room(s) size is (re) small to compare other kind similar product type of room(s) size. Although the prior property's price is cheaper to compare to the later properties. But, if some property buyers hoped the property has large room(s) size, then the later larger room(s) size which will be possible to some property buyer's preference choice. Even, their property price is more expensive to compare the smaller room(s) size of properties. Thus, the property's room size which will be one major factor to influence property buyers' purchase decision. room's size had relationship to facility management issue. Moreover, if the room's quality and design is attractive, then it will bring more attractive to persuade some property buyers to choose to buy them to live in preference.

Hence, whether the new property is good durable product feeling which will influence householder's choice. If the householder feels the new property has long term durable life to avoid to spend much maintenance expense when they have been living in the new property for a long term period. They will believe it has better facility management, quality to let them to live longer time and the most importance is that they do not need to spend any maintenance expense , due to the property 's any internal facilities are damaged easily.

The external factors may include: culture, reference groups, family, social class and demography of lifestyle as well as internal factors may include: feelings, past property buying and living experience , property knowledge, motivation of the property buyer individual psychology. These both factors can influence any property buyer individual decision making process to do final house purchase behavior. However, internal factors, such as: property knowledge of facility management and property living experience, e.g. how to evaluate to choose to buy the property , due to the property buyer's past living experience for the past property's facilities whether its facilities can satisfy its property buyers' comfortable living needs. This internal factor will be more important to influence any property buyer's property purchase final decision. If he/she feels whose prior old property's facilities are satisfactory. Then, he/she will compare this new property and old property's facilities to decide whether this new property is value to buy. So, the old property's facility will be the measurement standard to compare his/her next new property purchase choice. So, the property purchaser will compare these new and old property's property facilities product knowledge to similarities among property alternative which will influence his/her final decision to choose to buy the new property to live.

It seems that property low price factor must not guarantee to attractive many property buyers' choice. Otherwise, it is assumed that many property buyers like rent or buy to live the property for themselves for long term intention. There are less property buyers expect to sell the first property to earn profit intention. So, they will usually consider whether the property is long term durable product to avoid to pay maintenance expense when they had been living in the property in long term.

Some factors that taking consideration are proximity to the specific location, housing prices, developer's brand, the payment scheme, reference group, which are not the main factors to influence any property buyer individual choice. Because property buyer's need is that the property has good facilities to supply to them to live, e.g. good heater equipment can provide hot water to them to bath in winter or good air conditioners can provide cold temperature to let them to feel cool comfortable feeling in summer in their homes. Good electric tools facilities , when they have need to use electricity in safe environment at home, e.g. car park accessibility facility , level of security facility , surface area facility and housing types, bedroom, bathroom facilities, quality of housing manufacturing raw material, house design , house durable guarantee, speed of complaint responsiveness, specification accuracy, confirmation of building plan service, showing legal file property purchase process service, finance instalments process assistance, speed of responsiveness, officers' skills of presentation. All of above these concern property facility management issues will influence any property buyers' final choice to decide whether the property is value to buy. So, facility management will influence property purchaser individual final decision in possible.

● Hotel facilities influence hotel consumer choice

Travellers choose hotel to live. They will consider price, room comfortable feeling, hotel location , gum sport or entertainment service facility supplies , hotel room booking service etc. factors to decide whether the hotel can achieve every traveller individual minimum living need. However, whether hotel facilities factor will be the main factor to influence travellers' living needs. How and why do travellers consider hotel facilities whether are enough supply or facilities of quality to satisfy their demand to cause their living choice to the hotel final decision.

Usually, hotel's customers won't plan to live too long time, e.g. more than three months in the hotel. Because they are travelling aim. It will bring this question: Does hotel facilities quality consider to influence their hotel living choice if the traveller is short-term traveller to the country? However , some travellers who have effort to spend money to live high class hotels, even their journey is short trip. Hence it seems that short trip , hotel living reason can not influence the high class hotel travellers' living comfortable demand to the high class hotel room. Hence , the high class hotel room's facility management quality is also needed high performance. Even, when they need to eat breakfast, lunch , dinner in the high class hotel canteens or playing any sport equipment, or gum equipment or wathching movie in the hotel's small cinema room . They must need high class hotel can supply more entertainment, restaurant , sport facilities to satisfy their comfortable needs in the high class hotel. Moreover, they must consider safety issue when they are living in the high class hotel. So, thy must demand the hotel have enough five fright equipment in their rooms, or corridors and the stairs to let them can leave the dangerous locations to arrive the most safe locations immediately when the hotel has fire accident occurrence in any where . So, it ensures that the high class hotel's customers must ensure the high class hotel's facilities can satisfy their any one of above these needs before they decide to live this high class hotel.

In fact, high class hotel's room price must be more expensive to compare the low class hotel. So, it explains why high class hotel's consumers will need the hotel has safe and good quality of facilities to let them to feel it is one reasonable price, safe , good service and good facilities' high class hotel to live. Usually, when the traveller arrives the country to travel, the travelers chooses the hotel to live, it is whose first time visit in common. So, he/she ought consider that the hotel environment seems it is good or bad to let the traveller to select to live. If the hotel's facility environment is new and beauty and design colorful to let the first time travellers to feel. Then, it is possible that good facilities environment can influence the first time travellers to select to live, even the hotel's room price is more expensive to compare other similar hotels in the travelling living places. Hence, it explains why hotel facilities can influence traveller individual room booking choice. When he/she is the first time to visit the hotel to select whether to live or not.

● How and why facility management can influence workplace productivity to bring customer satisfaction

Facility management is one part of manufacturers or retailers as their productivity in workplace as their input and functionalistics within physical environment. In fact, facility management in workplace may include: site selection, property disposal, site acquisition, workplace space allocation, space inventory, space forecasting facility management, interior furniture change planning, interior furniture installation, moving maintenance, inventory, design evaluation, employment satisfaction evaluation plan, external maintenance and breakdown maintenance, preventive maintenance, landscape maintenance, energy space facility management, hazardous waste disposal, capital , operating furniture budgeting. So, it seems that one workplace considered whether the workplace's facility is enough to let employees to work in order to raise efficiency and improve productive performance more easily. Then, it will bring this question:

● How and why workplace facility management can influence consumer individual satisfaction?

Strategic FM delivery is essential for business survival. I shall explain why for delivery is important to influence customer satisfaction. In business process view point, an effective and meaningful service to their customer , i.e. the user. For logistic industry, the product's delivery time will influence when the product can be sent to the user's arrival destination. If the product is delayed to sent to the user's home or office or any location destination. The reason is because the logistic product sender has no efficient facility management (FM) arrangement in its warehouse . Then, its warehouse lacks efficient (FM), which will cause users to feel its delivery service is poor and they will complain its delivery service staffs. Then, they will find another delivery service company to replace its service. So, it explains that logistic industry's warehouse (FM) service arrangement can raise efficient time to send any products to their customers in order to let they feel satisfactory service. For example, Amazon online logistic company's warehouse has applied artificial intelligence robotic tools to assist warehouse workers to arrange the different kinds of products to deliver to the right shelves . Then, the warehouse robotics will follow their right product shelves locations to follow the right products to deliver to US domestic or overseas product buyers in the short time and it can avoid the wrong products to deliver to the wrong buyers' risk. Also, the (AI) delivery tools can raise time efficiency to assist Amazon warehouse workers to reduce their work load, and tried to work in large warehouse environment. Although, its warehouse's area is large, the (AI) tools facility can help them to deliver the different products to different shelves in the right locations , e.g. exact product number and the kinds of product to be delivered to the right country' client's shelf location in the warehouse. Also, it implies FM is very important to influence Amazon warehouse delivery efficiency and avoiding delivery wrong occurrence chance. For example, the shelf location belongs to US domestic customers, or the shelf location belongs to Japan customers, or the shelf location belongs to Hong Kong customers, or any other Asia or Western countries' different customers' locations. The warehouse's facility needs have different countries' shelves enough space to put and it also need enough space to let the (AI) tools, robotic delivery workers and human workers both to walk to different shelves locations easily and the different countries' shelves number needs to be calculated accurate. For example, it has how many client number will buy Amazon's the kind product per day. If it has above 5,000 to 10,000 China clients to buy the kind of product. Then, it will need to make judgement how many shelves are placed in the warehouse. So, it can avoid to lack enough shelves to put any different kinds of products to prepare to delivery to China clients in efficient time and it won't avoid to delay to deliver to their homes or offices or any locations in China.

Hence, such as Amazon logistic case, it explains why warehouse's space shelves number and area or locations facility management can influence workers or (AI) delivery tools how to move convenient and avoiding the delivery to the customer's wrong destination chance occurrence and shortening time to deliver products to its clients efficiently. Then, due to the delivering time is shorten and the wrong delivery destination's occurrence chance is also reduced , even it can avoid to deliver the product to wrong client's destination occurrence. Then, the logistic firm's clients will feel more satisfactory to its product sale delivery service and their complaints will be avoided. Hence, it explains effective warehouse (FM) space management service arrangement is essential to any logistic businesses nowadays.

● Facility management brings departmental benefits

Why do organizations need have facility management (FM) service? As above examples indicate that (FM) can improve workplace environment facilities, e.g. warehouse environment to let workers to raise efficiencies or improve performances, even it can influence consumers to raise satisfactory to it's services indirectly, also it can help organizations' equipment to be used long term to cause old and are needed to spend expenditure to maintenance or change new equipment in order to improve better quality . So , it can assist organizations to avoid to spend more expenditure for new equipment purchase or maintenance. All these issues will be facility management service's benefits to an organizations, which can concern raising customers' service satisfaction, raising efficiency or improving productive performance, raising productivity, reducing equipment or property maintenance or new alternation much of expenditure spending, office or warehouse or any workplace space planning arrangement .

However, every organization will need a facility manager or manage whose team effectively . When a facility manager begins to apply FM techniques to solve business problems. The case for FM is made. It is a simple matter of demonstrating a qualified return on the investment required. Every organization's success, FM operation of three key activities: they include: needing a proper understanding of the organization's needs, wants, drivers and goals and knowing when needs to review its changing circumstances, developing an effective facilities solution o support the organization's needs, wants , property drives and contribute to achieve its goals both short term and long term, achievement of reliable delivery of that solution in a managed, measured manner.

So, it bring one question: What are the influential factors to be followed the right direction to FM manager's strategic FM operational decision? The influencing factors may include: ownership, governance sector, complexity and perhaps of most significant, the size of the organization's property portfolio.

In fact, major occupiers feel FM service need, they are large corporate organizations and public service organizations. Their aims usually are to raise. The most marginal improvement in efficiency or effectiveness, these aims are the great significance. Major property occupiers will already have a facilities department or individuals performing the FM function with another department like property, finance or human resource, sale and marketing's facilities.

Usually these FM need occupiers who will encounter this problem: How can apply FM service systems and processes to be developed to improve reliable service delivery making use of the economies of scale, not suffering because of the size of the problem. This question will be facility manager individual concerning question: How to apply (FM) technique to solve the improvement reliable service delivery making use of the economics of scale problem for whose organization?

In reality much of external facilities management benefits to organizations, instead of raising efficiency, improving performance, raising productivity, reducing maintenance expenditure, e.g. energy saving, reducing natural resource waste, increasing local employment, improving supply chain management are all elements of the FM contribution to every organization's need. Hence are the work life balance argument and provision of an effective and safe working environment that supports why some organizations feel need (FM) service to support their organizational development.

Moreover, on cost benefit of space saving efficient view point, space service cost reduction is a key driver for all organizations and the medium, or large sized players will benefit directly from a well coordinated facilities strategy. For example, application FM technique to help warehouse or office space area to save 50% space vacancy to let employees can move easily or putting enough furniture or equipment or many stocks can be putted in warehouses . So, paying more rent expenditure to rent or purchasing another new warehouse or office to satisfy workers or employees' working environment to be better need. If the organization has effective (FM) technique, then it has enough space vacancy to supply to the increase stocks number to be putted inside in warehouse and it can let workers to move safety in available to let staffs to move easily and equipment have enough space to be stored in the limited warehouse space problem.

For greater space savings benefits will bring either long term renting or buying of increasing offices or warehouse number expenditure problem to any organizations, when the organizations' cost or renting or buying accommodation probably accounting for 60 to 70% of total occupancy cost . So a strategic program to release space or the prevent the acquisition of moves can be the most significant consideration to any facility manager, with between 40% and 60% of the workplaces are unoccupied in most offices or warehouses at any given moment in time.

Hence, how to apply (FM) technique to save space occupied areas for employment moving or stocks or equipment saving need in offices or warehouses. This issue will be any facility managers' seeking methods to solve problem. However, the important major advantage of facility management to organizations is that the application of management principle to keep the organization's property assets with the aim of maximizing their potentials. Thus, any organizations' facilities have become important, due to the property facilities' worth will increase if the organization's facility management technique can protect the organization's facilities have good performance. Then, the organization's maintenance expenditure will reduce and it won't need to spend expenditure to buy any new facilities to replace old facilities , due to they often damage factor when they are used old.

In conclusion, it explains why effective FM combines resources and activities can raise work environment improvement, which is essential to the raising employee performance aim. For hotel living service case example, this industry must need have good facility management service because hotels must need to fully equipped in term and facilities for effectiveness to satisfy hotel living clients' demand , hotels ought need good facilities asset management style lead to effectiveness in service delivery, there are benefit derivable from the adoption of facilities management from which other hotels can learn from for their effective operations. Hence, it explains why effective FM can bring benefits to hotels' properties to be more comfortable, beautiful appearances to attract many hotel customers to choose to live the hotel. Because hotel's building industrial kitchens, rooms facilities, equipment , halls of categories, restaurant facilities, gum sport entertainment centers' facilities, fans, elevators, lifts, electrical installation, escalators, baking equipment, recreational facilities, including golf courses which will be important factors to influence hotel clients' comfortable living feeling, if the hotel can keep its all facilities in the best living environment often. Then, it can raise chance to attract many hotel customers to choose it to live. So , hotel industry has absolute need to implement effective FM strategy to keep its properties more attractive to satisfy its clients' living needs.

Instead of hotel industry, logistic transportation industry also needs effective facilities management in warehouse, because of the logistic company's warehouse 's facilities are good, then it will assist to raise employee individual efficiency in the safe and system shelve stored facilities in workplace environment and improving performance.

Consequently, it will bring the shorten time to deliver any products to clients to avoide the delaying time delivery in order to let customers to feel more satisfactory to their services. In simple, it seems that some industries need have effective facilities management techniques to help them to bring long term customer satisfactory feeling, worker individual efficiency raising and performance improvement benefits. Hence, it seems facility management techniques' demand will be increased to some industries in popular in the future because it has help to raise employee individual efficiency , productive performance and client individual satisfactory level consequently.

Facility management how influences employee Psychology to raise productive efficiency

● How to impact of workplace
management on well-being and
productivity
In facility management strategy, design can lead promotion, the value of offices that are enriched, particularly including warehouses, shopping centers to raise their market value. Moreover, effective organizations, such as raising powering workers when giving the effective design of office space. I assume that a good design of an interior office workspace environment seems a psychological department to influence staff individual emotion to bring positive power in order to raising productive efficient influence, such as in a commercial city office. So, it brings this question: How workspace management strategy can impact on staff's working behaviors in office.

In fact, office tasks general include various forms of productivity, e.g. information processing, information management and any clerical tasks by computerization. Hence, office productivity concerns how to influence each office white color worker applies computers to work in office. The office space can impact on white color workers' performances in these several aspects: feeling of psychological comfort, organizational physical comfort and job satisfaction and productivity, efficiency. So, it seems that office workspace design strategy can influence white color workers' working behavior and attitude and performance indirectly.

The office space management includes: how to removal from the workspace of everything except the materials required to do the job at hand, how tight managerial control of the workspace, and how to implement standardization of managerial practice and workspace design. So, these key ideas will influence how each white color worker's efficiency and productivity in office working environment.

For this office space design situation, a large unseparated small space size's space design can accommodate more people and so brings itself to economies of scale. As a result, space occupancy can be centrally managed with minimal disruptive interference from office workers. Indeed, many businesses now adopt a clean and fresh air office working policy because they have more employees than they have spaces at which they can work. This desks are either taken on a first -come first -served basis. (hot desking) or can be booked in advance. So , when a company has many employees need to work in a small space working environment. It must concern how to let staffs to feel more comfortable in order to reduce high psychological pressure to work in this uncomfortable working environment. Hence, it explains why workspace design can impact on office workers' performance in some offices. All these issues are assumed that empowering workers to manage and have input into the design of their own workspace, then the effective office or any working places space management will enhance wellbeing to bring workers' positive emotions and improving productivity. I also assume the space working environment design have relationship of these depend variable factors to influence office worker individual productive efficiency. The variable factors may include psychological comfort, organizational comfortable, job satisfaction, physical comfort and productivity.

However, office furniture , facilities will influence office white color workers' performance ,e.g. the room size whether is big or small for manage office worker, a high backed, comfortable leather chair is needed for office staffs to sit down to let more comfortable, the door and most of the walls need glass, the office room environment needs have sea-grass rug beneath the desk covering the immediate working area, the office also needs have plants and pictures, mail boxes, telephone and computer facility is needed. When one staff needs to send email or phone call or send letters or deliver documents conveniently. These office elements are essential in order to increase physical well-being and feeling of satisfaction to white-color workers. Hence, geren office and office working space design management is needed in order to influence white color workers' productive efficiency in long term.

● Effective workspace design can influence communication to raise productivity

Office white-color workers often need communication between their managers, supervisors, and themselves. Office communication extends from the way that a user experiences a service. An effective office communication can bring these benefits; Providing positive influence on decision making by presenting a strong point of view and developing mutual understanding, delivering efficient decisions and solutions by providing accurate , timely and relevant information, enabling mutually benefit solutions, building health relationships by encouraging trust and understanding between the high level, middle level and low level staffs.

Effective office communication needs to clearly communicate its nature and purpose. Good communication ensures that all service staffs are sending out the same messages. Communication is also important for ensuring the service understands what users requires and why he/she talks about understanding users' needs and communication receiver can have effective communication skill to understand what he/she needs the another to do and the another knows he/she ought how to work by his/her task demand. Then, it will shorten much time. If the office has 100 staffs need to often communicate. However, if the office has good space management arrangement to let every staff can communicate easily and walks to anywhere to find the right staff to communicate conveniently. Then, they can spend less time to waste on communication issue. Then, their productive efficiency will be also influence to raise.

● Health and safe work environment influences productivity

Is a health and safe work environment can raise employees' work productive efficiencies indirectly? How and why it can influence employees' productive performance? Some occupations' working environments are easier to occur occupational accidents and diseases risks when the workers are working in the high health and safe risk's working environment. Hence, health and safety issues at these high life risk workplaces can be considered as a key to influence employees' overall performance. The idea that health and safety management program have positive impacts on productivity.

When one worker needs to work in this high risk of health and safe workplace. He/she will consider whether how his/her work behavior will bring suffer serious injuries for shorter or longer time from work related causes in possible. So, he/she will work carefully in order to avoid injuries occurrence chance. It is possible to influence whose work performance, low productive efficiency in order to avoid any occupational accident occurrences in the dangerous workplace.

If the employee feels danger when he/she needs to stay in the warehouses stable location to work often. Then his/her absenteeism day number will have increase, due to he/she feels that workplace accidents and occupational illnesses and can lead to permanent occupational disability, when he/she needs to attend the stable dangerous workplace to work in the warehouse. Hence, he/she will choose to apply holiday often in order to avoid injuries chance increasing when he/she needs to stay in the stable workplace location in the warehouse. It explains why companies increase need qualified, motivated and efficient workers who are able willing to contribute activity to technical and organizational innovations. So, healthy workers working in healthy working conditions are thus an important precondition for organization to work smoothly and productively. Hence, a health and safety workplace environment can bring these benefits to organizations as below:

It can prevent among workers of learning work, due to health problems caused by their working conditions, the protection of workers in their employment from risks resulting from factors adverse to health. The placing and maintenance of the worker in an occupational, environment adapted to his/her physiological and psychological, capabilities, mental , physical and social conditions of workplace and adequacy of health and safety measures are needed to any employees in order to bring positive impact not only on safety and health performance, but also productivity. However, identifying and quantifying these effects will difficult to be measured as well as the quality of a working environment has a strong influence on productive efficiency.

For one aviation air plane manufacturing factory, where workplace can environment will have high risk to occur occupational related accidents to cause employees' injuries. Hence, employees will be consider themselves safety when they need to work in high accident occurrence workplace. The bad consequence will influence such as absenteeism day number increases, leaving this kind of aviation air plane job of employees number increases, low productive efficiencies, due to there are many proficient experienced employees who choose leave this kind of high accident risk occupation.

Consequently, any high accident occurrence risk workplace environment , employers need have good safe and health strategy to let their employees have confidence to work in this kind of high risk accident occurrence workplace if they expect low productive efficiencies effect is caused by high accident occurrence risk workplace factor.

● Employee personal
empowerment factor influences
performance

Is empowerment one good method to raise employee himself/herself effort in order to improve productive efficiency in organizations. Empowerment often consists of support groups, e.g. management's effective leading or trainer's training, course educational opportunities. Employee self-management education may impact to improve himself/herself job performance, e.g. increased self-empowerment, self-management skills and job treatment satisfaction.

Only organization's empowerment strategy can lead every employee to through improvements in the employee individual decision making efficacy, improvement task performance behavior by reviewing whether what are the employee himself/herself errors when he/she encounters any job difficulties, after he/she reviewed his/her task error and his/her manager feels his/her performance can be improved. Then, it can enhance satisfaction with the employee and his/her manage relationship and better access and raising efficient performance in possible . Hence, empowerment can let every employee to discover whether what task related difficulties he/she faces or encounters every day. When his/her manager give ideas to let him/her to know how he/she ought review his/her task error in a supportive education working environment, it aims to let the low performance or low inefficient employees to increase confidence to continue work in the organization. So, the employee turnover number will decrease , if the inefficient employees can feel that they can attempt to solve their task-related difficulties successfully by themselves. So, empowerment can increase social support, leadership and advocacy development , it has resulted in greater employee individual performance psychological empowerment, autonomy and authority to let every employee to feel to achieve to improve themselves efficiencies more effectively in any organizations.

For hospital organizational efficiency measurement empowerment influence case, how empowerment can influence hospital's efficiency raising? Efficiency is one of the most important indicators of hospital performance evaluation. Why do some hospitals' efficiencies poor? It is possible that mis management of resources, lacking health plan packages, e.g. coverage of basic health insurance, poor quality of care service, more payment demand for out-of pocket payment , quality of primary healthcare , healthcare providers neglect to concern potentially about service efficiency issues.

In fact, low hospital efficiency is the major problem to influence patients number to choose the hospital's medical service, e.g. when the hospital often needs patients to queue to wait for doctor's care medical service. They need to wait on hour at least or more when the hospital has many patients are waiting for its medical service. Then, it will influence them to choose another hospital to replace it , if the hospital 's medical fee is cheaper and it does not need patients to spend long time to queue to wait its medical service. So, service efficiency is important to influence patients consumers' positive or negative feeling to choose the hospital's medical service. Even, the hospital's doctors are famous or they own many medical working experience, if patients often need long time to queue to wait its medical service . Then, it will cause its patients number to be reduced .

These are variable factors to influence the hospital's inefficiency. They may include old speed hospital information system and medical record documents based on inefficient input and output variables. Input variables may include the number of hospital admissions, the number of nurses and the number of available beds. The output variable may include average of length of stay and bed turnover interval inefficient paper document record in the patient record administrative department.

However, to evaluate the hospital efficiency indicators may include technical, scale and managerial efficiency the out-based data development analysis approach and the variable returns to scales assumption was used. Based on the out-input based approach (maximizing the factors of medical service production), to increase efficiency the organization should be increased outputs.

Hence, when the hospital has good efficient evaluation method to measure every staff's performance , e.g. ward administrative clerk, patient registration clerk etc. Then, it can base on an put-put based approach and assuming a variable return to scale, there is capacity to improve technical efficiency and managerial efficiency in these any hospital different administrative units without an increase in costs and use of same amount of resources in relation to technical efficiency and managerial efficiency and scale efficiency of hospital's administrative labour individual task.

In conclusion, factors, such as modification of managerial practices, use of modern technologies tailored to the cultural, political and formulation of clinical guidelines to standardize the medical processes in order to reduce medical errors and increase the empowerment of health care buyers (insurance organizations), length of stay, management hospitals by specialist managers, administrative requirement, full time hospital physicians, limiting the authority of decision makers in relation to the recruitment of staff in accordance with the needs of the hospital and optimal allocation of beds, conducting economic evaluations and the type of hospitals ownership had an impact on the hospital efficiency significantly. By increasing the number of beds the hospitals efficiency decreases. Otherwise, optimizing the bed size can increase hospital efficiency.

However, the important factor to raise hospital overall staffs efficiencies empowerment is needed to let every hospital staff to review whether why and how himself/herself error is caused and he/she needs to review his/her errors to avoid to be caused from any negligence again in order to avoid patients' complaints again or reduce the patients' complaint number aims. So, empowerment of staff himself/herself error review factor is one major raising efficient good method.

● How organizational facility environment factor influences new and old employees long term performance

In psychological view ,in any organization's environments, they depend on the types of social and physical environment factors to influence employee personal behavior how to be caused. How and why does the employee select to do whose behavior? If the organization's physical and social environment is better, then it may influence its employees select to work hard. It is possible to bring productive efficient raising consequence.

In fact, when one new employee enters the new organization to work, he/she needs to learn how to adapt to cooperate with the organization's old employees to work together. So, it explains how and why organization's physical and social environment can influence the new employee individual motivation of behavior to work. In regarding new employee individual behavior by new employer's culture expectations as well as new employees need to adapt of actions that are likely to productive positive outcomes and generally discard those that bring unrewarding or puniishing outcomes by new employer's treatment.

However, anticipated material and organization environment co-operation outcomes between the new employee and the organization old employees' cooperation, which are not the only kind of incentives that influence the new employee behavior of the new employee actions were performed only on behalf of anticipated external rewards and punishment from the new employer. In actuality, the new employee concerns considerable self-direction in the face of the new employer's organization's old employees competing influences. However, when the new employee has adopted an intension and an action plan. When, he/she works in the new organization for a period, he/she can't simply not back and visit for the appropriate performances to appear.

The new employee's new job goal will be motivated by enlisting self-evaluative engagement in activities rather than directly. By making self-evaluation conditional on matching personal new job standards, the new employee will give direction to his/her new job pursuits and create self-inventions to sustain his/her efforts for new job goal attainment. The new employee will select to do new task behavior to give him/her self-satisfaction and a sense of pride and self worth for the new job chance.

Efficacy beliefs also play a key role in shaping the new employees' behavior to do their tasks by influencing the types of new organization's activities and working environments, the new employees choose to set into any factor that influences the employee's choice behavior can affect the direction of employee personal career development in the new organization. This is because the organizational working environment influences operating in the employee how to select working environments continue to work. Thus, by choosing and shaping the new organization's working environments, new employee can have a hand in what they expect.

In conclusion , when a new employee chooses the new organization to work. He/she must need to adapt the organization's new working environment. If he/she feels difficult to adapt or accept to the organization's new working environment, then he/she will be influenced to work inefficient or poor productive performance , due to he/she feels unhappy to work the new organization's working environment and the new organization's manager will dissatisfy his/her performance and complain or give verbal warning to dismiss him/her. Then, it will bring the poor consequence to let the organization's inefficient productive performance effect. If many new employees feel difficult to adapt to work in the new organization. Then, inefficient productive performance will be influenced to keep a long term. So, it implies that the organization will need to change its organizational culture in order to let many new employees can adapt and accept this new organizational culture to work happily if the organization expects new employees work to raise productive efficiency successfully.

● Raising efficient and effective
interview psychological methods

In human resource department, interviewing and selecting the most right applicants to do different kinds of positions, it is one part of HRM function. If the interviewer need to spend more time to interview to decide whom is the most right applicant to do the position in one day, e.g. 50 at least , even more applicants number as well as he/she can also make the more accurate personal selection decision to choose the most right applicant to do the position after the interview day. Then, the interviewing process needs to be avoided to spend more time to choose the most suitable applicant to do the position within the day. It is difficult to judge whether whom ought be the most right applicant to do the position, if there are more than 50 applicants , they are needed to be interview in the day. The consequence will bring HR department can spend extra time to do the interview task, but it can have enough staffs and time and resource to do other urgent or important task at the interview day. It will bring this question: How to apply psychological method to raise interviewer's efficiency to shorten to spend extra time to do interviewing tasks ? I shall explain some psychological methods to attempt to let interviewers have more confidence to select the most right applicant in short time as below:

1. Behavioral interview skill

The interviewer can apply the actual behavioral interview method to let the interviewee to answer how he/she deals the matters, he/she feels that it is the best decision in order to judge and analyze whether whom applicant is the most suitable to be selected, e.g. describing the situation, he/she needs or the task that he/she needs to accomplish. The situation may be from a previous job, any relevant event, describing the action he/she took and be sure to keep the focus on him/her , e.g. discussing a group project or effort in the team; explaining what results he/she achieved, what happen? How did the event and what dis the applicant accomplishes? What did the applicant learn?

In the behavioral-based interview. the interviewer can need the applicant to attempt to explain examples clearly in order to judge whose analytical skill whether he/she is the suitable applicant to do the position. The interviewer may ask the applicant to identify some examples from whose post experience where he/she demonstrated top behaviors and skills that employers typically seek. To judge whether his/her examples should be totally positive, such as accomplishments or meeting goals, the other half should be situations that started at negatively , but either ended positively or he/she made the best of the outcome.

This behavioral interview test aims to review whether the applicant's every example answer, he/she can provide an appropriate description of how he/she demonstrated the desired behaviors. In the behavioral interview, the interviewer can attempt to judge whether the applicant has good imagine effort to mind any relatively small set of examples to respond to a number of different behavioral questions to satisfy the right example are applied to the right situations in the limited interview time. Hence, behavioral interview can let the interviewer to make more accurate analysis to judge whether whom applicant(s) has (have) good analytical effort to solve any work-related situational problems in the most reasonable way or attitude in order to select whom is the most right applicant to do the position.

2. E-mail interviewing in qualitative research

E-mail interviewing is another good interview method to select right applicant to do the managerial level position. E-mail interviewing can be in many cases a viable alternative to face-to-face telephone interviewing. Internet-based qualitative research methods may include online personal interview and virtual focus groups. However, it brings two questions: What opportunities and challenges does online in depth interviewing present for collectively qualitative data? How can in depth e-mail interviews be conducted effectively?

The applicant targets may be the top-level manager, advertising executive , sales manager, human resource manager etc. management position applicants. They need to answer any complex or difficult interviewing question by email in the limited time, e.g. how to solve one case study problem , how to give recommendation to solve the situation problem. The interview participants may be recruited by tool/method of psychological test questions, the interview questions may be interview guide in a single e-mail and follow yp, length of email data collection period may be up to 10 weeks, the number of e-mail or follow up exchanges may be several number. The electronic formal and require little editing or formation before the applicants are processed for analysis all e-mail interviewing questions. So, they need to answer any managerial case study problem in limited time. It is one good managerial interview test method to evaluate whether whom applicant has the best analysis effort in order to the managerial position, because they need to find the best solutions to give recommendations to attempt to solve any situational problems in any un predictive case study problems. For example, when the applicant or a focus group of discussion applicants whom need to spend the maximum half hours to give recommendations to discuss to solve one complex or difficult case study problem either between the interviewer and the another interviewee applicant or between the group of five to ten interviewees (job applicants) themselves. Thus, after the interviewer sent the one case study question to let the applicants to know by every email channel. The interviewer needs to judger whether whom one applicant or one of the focus group applicants their recommendations are the most reasonable to solve the case study managerial situational problem within half hour to one hour. Then, the interviewer can make more accurate judgement to select whether whom has the best analytical effort to do the managerial position.

3. The effectiveness of motivational interviewing for young or older adult applicants selection process

How can apply case management skills to be effective to prepare any interview motivation? How to do the most effective and efficient to meet the objectives of the interview? Some interview techniques used may vary the based on the individuals involved in the interview. For an interview with the young age applicant more require a different approach than an interview with a senior adult applicant. The following are one pointers to assist with preparing for the interview as below:

Knowing the purpose of the interview and what needs to be accomplished . What is the expected outcome? Gathering all forms that need to be completed or signed having the interview and making list of questions that need to be asked, knowing the key facts and topics to be discussed, during the interview. Gathering factual information that may be helpful. Opening mind is needed in the whole interview process. Making an appointment for the interview and arranging sufficient time to set fully participate in the interview. Taking notes during the interview, let the participants know in general terms the reason notes are being made and how they will be used, opening ended questions invite the applicant to provide more information usually begin with other words who, what, where, how, asking one question at a time and keeping wording simple and specific, defining any terms that may be unfamiliar to the applicant , giving the interviewing participants in the interview an opportunity to ask their one questions or to clarify anything that was discussed, closing the interview with a review of the information discussed and facts gathered, reviewing any follow-up that is to be done by the case manager or others involved in the interview.

In an efficient and effective interview, the interviewer needs have good body and spoken word communication to the interviewee or the position applicant. Because a good communication can reduce waste time or avoid the extended longer interview time if the interviewer can make good communication to impact good message to let the applicant to understand what is the mean to his/her interview question. What he/she wants to know, the total impact of a message includes ,e.g. 7 % verbal (words), 38% vocal /volume, pitch, rhythm etc. and 55% body movements (mostly facial expression). The interviewer's body and verbal behavior can make more clear message to let the interviewee(job applicant) to understand what answers are he/she wants to know mostly. Hence, an efficient and effective interview can let the interviewer to control and manage the whole interview to evaluate whether whom the applicants' answers or feedbacks are more reasonable to be acceptable to be better to compare other applicants to apply the position more accurately.

● What is efficient achievement of technological inputs factor in construction industry

What is organizational efficient raising actual mean? I shall indicate construction industry case to explain technological factor is the major factor to assist construction organization to raise efficiency. For construction industry example, improved productivity could be attributed to advances in and increased usage of information technologies, increased competition, due to globalization and changes in workplace and organizational structures.

For construction efficiency, the construction process can reduce waste in coordinating labor and in managing, moving and installing materials, loss avoidance. It can achieve efficient aim. The construction productive efficient concept can be defined efficiency improvements as ways to cut waste and labor. So, one construction organizational efficient achievement means that it implemented through the capital facilities sector, these activities would significantly advance construction efficiency and improve the quality, timeliness, cost effectiveness of projects in construction processes.

On construction industry technological factor influence hand, it can influence that construction productivity how well, how quality, and at what cost buildings and infrastructure can be constructured, directly affects prices for homes and consumer products and the robustness of the national economy. Construction productivity will also affect the outcomes of national efforts to renew existing infrastructure systems; to build new infrastructure for power from renewable to renew existing infrastructure systems; to build new infrastructure for power from renewable resources to develop high-performance " green building" and to remain competitive in the global market. If the construction organization expected to achieve effficient aim. It ought consider how to change in building design, construction and renovation and in building materials and materials recycling, will be essential to the success of national efforts to minimize environmental impacts, reduce overall energy use, and reduce greenhouse gas emissions.

However, construction industry analysts differ on whether construction industry productivity is improved by efficiency outcome. They indicate construction efficiency needs to reduce 25-50 percent waste in coordinating labour and in managing, moving and installing materials. This is the most minimum standard efficient achievement level to any construction organizations.

What are the factors influence efficiency to any construction organizations? An efficient construction task process is made possible by a range of information technological tools and applications, including computer-aided design and drafting, three and four dimensional visualization and modeling programs, laser scanning, cost-estimating and scheduling tools and materials tracking. So, high technological tool will assist to raise efficient construction process to any construction organizations. It can help them to shorten time and avoid materials waste and control cost effective estimation for any construction projects.

Effective use of interoperate technologies requires effective team cooperative processes and effective planning up front and this it can help overcome obstacles to efficiency created by process fragmentation. Interoperable technologies can also help to improve the quality and speed of any construction project related decision making, integrate processes, managing supply chains, sequence work flows, improve data accuracy and reduce the time spent on data entry, reduce design and engineering conflicts and the subsequent need for rework, improve the life-cycle management of buildings and infrastructure.

All of these factors will influence whether the construction organization can implement efficiency in success. For example, interoperable techcholgies include legal issues, data-storage capacities and the need for " intelligent " search applications to sort quickly through thousands of data elements and make real-time information available for on-site decision making. How to improve job-site efficiency through more effective interfacing of people, processes, materials ,equipment, and information. The job site for a large construction project is a dynamic place, involving numerous contractors, subcontractors, trades people and labors, all of whom must require equipment, materials and supplies to complete their tasks. So, they need to know how to manage activities and demands to achieve the maximum efficiency from the limited available resources. Time, money, and resources will have possible to be wasted when projects are poorly managed, causing workers to have to wait around for tools and work crews are not on-site at appropriate time or when supplies and equipment are stored in complexity or difficulty, requiring that they can be moved multiple time (time waste).

How to improve job site safety and improve the quality of projects, significantly cut waste? The use of automated equipment, e.g. for excavation and earthmoving operations, pip installation, concrete placement, and information technologies, e.g. radio-frequency identification tags for tracking materials personal digital assistants for capturing field data. These high technological tool can help any construction projects to raise efficiency to process improvements and the provision for real -time information for improved management at the job site.

Moreover, on mannal research and development tools hand, instead of data technological tools hand, any construction organizations also need to consider how to take a variety of forms: How to test field on a job site? How to arrange lecture shows in efficient way, seminrs, training and conference, and scientific laboratories time, human resource available arrangement, spending expenditure budget to finish. Moreover, effective performance mearements are enablers of innovation and of corrective actions throughout a construction project's life cycle. They can help any construction companies or organizations understand how processes led to success or failure, improvements or inefficiencies and how to use that knowledge to improve construction products , processes and outcomes of active projects.

The nature of construction projects, the industry itself, any construction organizations ought consider the construction working environment how to influence construction workers' emotions. For example, when the construction site is high levels, of noise, dust and airborne particles, adverse weather conditions,and other factors that can cause injuries and thereby reduce efficiency and productivity. New types of equipment can make an active physically easier to perform, easier to control, move precise , and safer for construction workers. Similarly, changes in materials can reduce the weight of construction components, make them easier to handle, move and install. Manufacturing building components off-site providers need more control conditions and allow for improved quality and precision in the fabrication of the component, One study that examined the relationship between changes in material technology and construction productivity based on 100 construction a related tasks, the study found that labor productivity for the same activity increased by 30 % at least when higher materials were used and labour productivity also improved when construction activites were performed using materials that were easier to install or were pre-fabricated. So, it seems material heavy can influence construction worker individual productive efficiency in site, if the material is higher , then the construction worker's productivity will be influenced to improve (Goodrum et al. 2009).

Thus, the factors influence construction organization's efficiency. It focuses on whether the construction firm applies how advanced construction technologies to assist its construction workers to work as well as whether its construction environment can let workers to feel safe to avoid life danger or accident occurrence. When the workers do not worry about whose life safety as well as they can apply advanced construction technology to assist them to work. Then, their productive efficiencies ought need to be improved easily. Thus, facility management and advanced technology will be the main factor to raise construction workers' efficiencies.

Reference

Becker, F. (1990). " Facility management : a cutting edge field?" property management 8 (2): 25-28.

Bernard, M.B. & Bruce, J. A. (1994) Improving organizational effectiveness through transformational leadership: US. Sage publications, Inc. pp. 11-13.

Fiona, M.W. (2004). organizational behavior and work , a critical introduction, 2 ed. : New York, US, Oxford university press, pp.79 .

Jac, F.E.& John , R.M. (2014) predictive analytics for HRM:US Pearson Education pp.13-16

Stephen, P.R. & Timothy, A.J. (2018). Essentials of organizational behavior, 14 ed.: US. Pearson Education, Inc. pp.108-110.

CHAPTER FOUR

WHY SOCIAL BEHAVIOR MAY INFLUENCE ORGANIZATIONAL STRATEGY NEEDS TO BE CHANGED

Human Behavioral network job brings social economic benefits

What does human network job mean ? Why may human network job be popular? Why human network job behavior may influence economy ? Nowadays internet is popular to use. We can apply internet to find data , search any new things, even earn money. Why does internet may become huma network job source. For example, e-publish may be one kind of new human network job. Any authors may apply internet channel to help them to sell electronic or paper books from e-publisher web store. They may apply facebook, you tub etc. any online channel to promote themselves new books to let new readers to know whether when they may buy themselves favourable new topic books to read from electronic publisher web store.

Thus, future electronic publisher industry may help any authors to build internet network platform to help them to sell and promote
ot advertise their any one new electronic or paper book topic to let global any one reader to choose to buy their any new topic books from electronic publisher web store easily and conveniently. However, it implies that electronic network platform author may be one kind of future new human network job in our societies.

How electronic network platform author job may bring economy benefit in macro economy view? A person can have few friends, contacts and still be very influential if these few
friends and contacts are themselves highly influential, e.g. one author must not need to know any one reader in global society. When they like to choose any electronic books from electronic internet network platform. They may become the author's any one topic book buyer, when they feel the author's any one topic book is fun and attract they make decision to buth the strange author whose the topic book from electronic book publisher's platform web store conventiently in short time. Although, they are strangers, they do not know themselves , but the reader can understand what it way that made Google from writing platofrm to create new creative mind and typing network job method to replace traditional hand writing book method for global authors. It will be one kind of new human network writing job.

Hence, global any one reader can apply an innovative search engine , such as google.com to find whether whom author personal new topic books are value to read from internet.
Then, the electroniuc publisher's web store may be new book store platform sale network to help the author to sell many electronic or paper books from electronic network platform
in short time. So, internet may be future new network plaform to help global any one author to create network writing job absolutely. Furthermore, internet may be popular social media
to help any one author to build goold relationship between his/her readers. It is one kind of new network, human network job. New authors do not need to buy many paper books to prepare to put in any one book shop warehouse. Their every book can print on demand to reduce out of book stock in any one book shop. They may choose to sell either electronic books or paper books both from any one book publisher web store. So, electronic network platform may be one kind of good writing channel to help human authors to create income and it can also help authors to bring new creative mind and

new topic fun content books to let readers to know and buy to read from electronic publisher network platform.

Why does human behavior may be one kind of new human network job to bring global economic advantages. ALthough, it may be free income or without inocme, but the person does the network behavior, his/her behavior may be bring advantages to influence many other people's health. For this case, when a worker in a coffee shop in an airport gets a vaccination againinst the flu, it does not only helps him or her stay healthy, but also helps the many travellers who might otherwise have been inflected if that workers caught the flu. So, the externality , the result implies the vaccination of even a part of a community conveys benefits to the whole community. For example, governments pay special attention to the vaccinations of school children, teachers, health mothers, and the elderly, categories of people particularly susceptible not only to catching, but also to transmitting a disease.

It is not accidential that governments are heavily involved with vaccination . When there are externalities, free market, fail to persuade individual incentives with society's
their the worker's decision of whether to get a vaccine ends up attracting whether other people get sick. The workers might not fully take all these other people's potential suffering into account when making her or his vaccination decision.

As Stanford University does many suggestions, understand this and tries to help them make the right decisions and so providers free flu vaccines for its staff and students.
Small pockets of unvaccinated individuals can allow a disease to gain a spread more widely well-being. For example, parent weighing the costs and benefits of a vaccine for their child is not always thinking of the consequences of that vaccination to other people. THese are markets in which subsidizing or regulating behavior can make everyone better off. Because the reason for requiring that a child be vaccinated before enrolling in school is not just to protect that child, because each child's vaccination affects others via potential contagions.

Robots take our jobs behavioral and economy influences

Robot job behavior brings economy influences

If one day robots can replace human to do simple, even complex jobs. They will bring what influences to our global societial economy.The popular

economic refrain declares that the
global middle class is dying and robots will soon take our jobs, e.g. shopping center customer service jobs, library service jobs, cinema ticket sale jobs, restaurant kitchen cooker jobs,
even, bus drivers, taxi drivers etc. public transport driving jobs, accountant, doctors etc. professional jobs. Whether it is beautiful or petty matter if our future societies have many human jobs can be replaced to do from robots. Businessman must may reduce to employ employees and reduce to pay salary or wage, when robots can be replaced to do their employees tasks. But, societies must bring unemployement rate rises , due to societies will have many people loss jobs when their employers choose to buy robots to serve their clients or do any office tasks or customer service or cleaning etc. tasks.

In micro economy view, employers may save money in long term, but in macro economy view, it will cause unemployment ratio rises , even crime rate rises when there are many people lose
jobs in societies. These models of doom, though, fail to account for the hundreds of businesses riding the waves of change in their industries when robots may be invented to replace human to do many simple , even complex tasks in our future societies.

WE may image that one small factory needs to manufacture fishes canes to sell to supermarket, the small , cheaper stuff and higher margin parts of the fishes manufacture industry. Before, this factory needs to employe many human factory workers need to help every fresh customer makeing the perfect fishing gear, designed for performance, durability, and cost in order to achieve to manufacture every fish cane in whole fished processing manufacturing stages. Every worker needs to spend about 15 to twenty minutes to finish every fish cane , till to delivery to any supermarket to sell. If this fish canes manufacturing factory can apply manufacturing robots to help them to finish any one working tasks , every robot can only spend five minutes to finish whole fresh fish cane manufacturing process. Thus, every robot can
help this factory save 10 to 15 minutes time to finsh every fish cane manufacturing process. IN fact, time is money, because when every robot can help this factory to reduce 10 to 15 minutes time to compare human worker. Then, this factory can finish about 20 fish canes in one hour if it can use robot to help it to manufacture fish canes. Otherwise, if this factory still use human workers to help it to manufacture fish canes, then

it can finsh about 3 to 4 fish canes in one hour. SO, the manufacturing efficiency ensures that robots must help this fish manufacturing factory to raise fish canes number more than human workers. So, in robotic behavioral economy view, manufacturing robots must help this fish canes manufacturing factory to raise fish canes manufacturing number and deliver increasing number to supermarkets to prepare to sell every day. Robots can help this fish canes manufacturing factory bring manufacturing time saving, rising manufacturing efficiency, improving performance and reducing wages expenditure long time advantages in micro economy view. However, manufacturing robots can also bring disadvanages to society, e.g. increasing unemployment ratio, increasing crime rate,

this factory workers will lose jobs and income, they need earn social welfare from government and increasing government finance pressure in short time, even long time in macro economic view.

Stanford University graduate program in economics, Scott lecturer explained that "in demand and supply economic theory for robots supply and demand case, robots supply number increasing may influence human workers demand number decrease. It sometimes calls " the efficient frontier".

No specific human beings were mentioned in any of economics classes. As robots supply and demand in market case, They (robots) may be purely theoretical " agents" who reached to the most reasonable sale prices in order to persuade any one businessman buyer to make manufacturing robot buying decision whether robots can help him / her to bring how much saving time , saving money, saving cost, improving performance, efficiency economic benefit before he/she plans to reduce workers number when he/she decides to apply robots to replace human workers in his/her factory or office or any service department, e.g. cinema ticket sale service, shopping center customer service, shopping center cleaning , supermarket customer service etc. service or sale tasks. When robots can replace human to do any one of these tasks in any organizations. So, robots may be human worker agents who reached to prices the way robots would react to a software

command. There was nothing that explained why some people thrived and others did n't or why truly brilliant, hardworking people could fail when much lazier folks succeeded." Having been admitted to the Stanford University graduate program in economics, Scott lecturer hoped to get his answers there.

How robots influence our future social changing? Using the right technology can be a boon to your business in this economy. For internet example, it is easier than ever to find well-matched customers all around the world, to stay in contact with them, and to more quickly design the products they want. If you focus solely on being cutting -edge, though you risk letting the technology

take over what should be very robust relationships with your customers , employees, and colleagues. IN nowaddays society, technoligical advances and cutomation, personal

relationships in business are more crucial than ever. I mean that robots can not replace human to serve clients to let them to feel more comfortable and passion more easily. For shoe shop case example, if the shoe shop apply one robot to serve its clients to replace human shoe salesperson to serve its shoe customers. Robots ensure that they can not persuade every shoe potential buyer to make shoe buying decision more easily when robots need to contact every shoe potential buyer. The reason is simple, because robots can not touch any one shoe buyer individual emotion very easier.

If the shoe buyer needs the robots to help him/her to choose any right shoe styles when he/she can not feel himself / herself can make the most right shoe style choice decision. The robots can not replace human shoe salesperson to make shoe style choice judgement more easily. They must need longer time to analyze whether which shoe style may be the most suitable to the shoe buyer. Otherwise, human shoe salesperson may attempt to make the most right shoe style choice decision to help any one shoe buyer to chooce the most right style shoe because he/she owns shoe style sale experience, shoe style knowledge, the most important reason is that they can feel every shoe customer individual emotion to touch whether he/she will feel comfortable or happy when they attempt to help every shoe customer to seek the most right shoe style in every shoe customer whole shoe searching processing. Othwerwise, serving robots are only one machine, they can not touch or feel every shoe customer individual emotion whether he/she feel comfortable or unhappy or happy when they need to contact them in whole shoe searching processing. Hence, I believe that some tasks robots can

not repalce human staff to do very easily. Otherwise, robots may bring disadvanatges to let any one businessman to loss his/her customers, due to robots can not touch every customer

emotion to compare human staff in service tasks more easily. Robots serving customer behaviors may cause money lose and customers number lose to the shop in micro economic view.

Intellectual human economic behaviors

What does intellectual human economic behaviors mean ? I believe that when we choose or decide to do intellectual behaviors, then our societies will be influenced to bring economic growth in consequence.I shall attempt to indicate pollution case to explain how and why eithet our intellectual or foolish behaviors may bring economic growth or recession in consequence as below:

On one hand, for air pollution social case aspect example, if we only consider to buy cars to drive for working aimr or holiday leisure aim. Then, our societies air will be polluted. Our health will be influenced to bad. Our car driving behaviors may cause global environment air pollution serously. In long tiem, global air pollution will bring our bodies health to be bad. Although, ourselves car driving behaviors may bring our driving travelling leisure enjoyment and comfortable feeling in short time, also we so not need to pay public transport fare often, but we need to compensate ourselves health economic intangible loss due to air pollution , when cars number increases, dirty air will cause ouselves health to become bad.

In the result, we will need to pay more medical expenditure when we are old age, due to ourselves bodies will become bad, due to we breathe global dirty air every day, due to ourselves cars pollute air in long time, e.g. 10 to 20 years, even 30 more without limited air pollution environment. So, driving cars behavior may be one kind of human foolish behavior and our foolish behavior may bring ourselves future long time medical expenditure absolutely.

One the other hand, water pollution social aspect, if we often keep much rubblish to pollute sea, oil exploration porcessing pollute ocean , ships gas pollute ocaen, then fishes will eat polluted food and drive dirty water, due to global ocean is polluted.

In fact, because human only to conside how to buy boats to carry on leisure enjoyment activities, or catch cruises to travel on the sea. Also, oil manufacturers only consider researching anywhere to find new oil exploration places to manufacture oil product, when their oil exploration processes pollute ocarn . Consequently, global fishes drink polluted warer or eat polluted food. They will have poison. SO, human will have high chance to eat poison polluted fishes, due to fishes are poison or are polluted. So, human is doing foolish activities, we only hope to find oil exploration places to pollute ocean or we only spend money to buy ticket to catch ships to travel anywhere in global ocean. All of these human foolish behaviors will bring pollution to global ocean. On consequently, we will need to compensate to eat polluted or dirty or poision fishes, ourselves bodies health will be bad. In long time, we need have high chance to pay medical expenditure when we are old. So, pollution case may be one good example to explain how and why human foolish behavior may influence ourselves future need to compensate serious medical loss.

All of these human foolish behavior will bring pollution to global ocean. On consequently, we will need to compensate to eat polluted or dirty or poison fished , ourselves bodies health will be bad. In long time, we will have high chance to pay medical expenditure, when we are old. So, pollution case may be one good example to explain how and why human ourselves intellectual or foolish behaviors may influence future long time economic loss or economic growth or recession in micro and micro economic view.

On another water pollution aspect hand, if we often keep rubbish to sea, oil exploration processing pollutes ocean and ships' gas pollute ocean, then fishes will eat polluted food and drink dirty water, due to fishes will eat polluted food and drink dirty sea water because the global ocean is polluted seriously.

In fact, because human only consider how to buy boats to carry on any leisure water activities, or catches cruises to travel on the sea. Also, oil manufacturers only consider any where to find oil exploratin places to manufacture oil products from ocean, when their pol exploration processes can plooute ocean. Consequently, global fishes drink polluted water or eat direty food. They will have poison. So, human will have high chance to eat poison fishes.

Otherwise, such as pollutin case, it can infuence inflation or deflation. Consequently, the reason indicates supply and demand theory. If air pollution is serious, then we will consider health issue, global cars demand number may be influenced to reduce, when global cars number demand will reduce, global car prices and supply number will need to change to fall down in order to attract or persuade global car consumers choose to make car purchase decision.

Hence, global car manufacture number and car price will be influenced to reduce, due to global air pollution issue. Consequently, deflation will occur because when the country citizen usually does not spend much extra saving money to buy car expensive goods. Money value will be low. Otherwise, if global cair pollution is not serious, human considers to buy cars to enjoy driving leisure lives. So, global car demand is influenced to increase , also global car price will also influenced to increase.

Consequently, gobal human will choose to buy cars to drive. Due to we accept to spend extra saving to buy expensive car goods. Car sale price and supply may be influenced to rise up. Money value is influenced to reduce. Inflation may be influenced, due to global car consumers number increases, we would not have extra money to spend easily. Car expensive goods expenditure influences our spending habit to avoid to make car purchase decision more easily. So, human intellectual or foolish activities may bring inflation or deflation consequency in possible indirectly in macro economic view.

On conclusion, above pollution case explain that how and why human intellectual or foolish economic behaviors may bring inflation or deflation consequency as wll as economic growth or recession consequency as well as any goods demand and supply increasing or decreasing consequency. It implies that human behavior may have indirect relationship to influence any goods demand and supply number to either increase or decrease result as well as any goods price will be influenced to increase or decrease in micro and macro economic view.

The relationship between social change and human behavior

Why does economic changes may influence human individual behavioral change? I shall attempt to indicate shopping behavior and staying at home behavior to explain their case and effect relationsip as below:

Human behavior can be influenced by economic change or economic change can be influenced by human behavior? Why does recession may influence consumers reduce shopping desire? In social recession suitation, it is possible that many people lose jobs suddenly, due to businessmen lose many customers. They need to make decision to reduce employees number in order to continue to keep businesses. Consequently, many firms (organizations) their employees may lose jobs. When they have much time, due to lose jobs, they will feel to avoid to spend too much time and money to go to shopping often. Many losing jobs people, they will often stay at homes. So, they will reduce time to go to shopping, then non essential products won't their preferable choice purchase products. Hence, recession will change many losing jobs people their shopping or consumption desires to avoid to buy non essential products often . Usually when economic boom, many people have jobs to do because consumers number must increase when many people have jobs to do. Then, many people can accept to spend money to buy non essential products often. Many people feel spend time to go to shopping can satisfy their purchase of any kinds of new products useful psychology or desire. So, recession is one good example to explain it can influence many people do not like often to leave homes to go to shopping easily. Many people like to stay at homes, becaue they feel worry about spending too much shopping time when they leave homes. Their staying home time is one good negative shopping behavior example. So, economic change may influence human individual behavior changes , they have direct cause and efect relationship in behavioral economic view.

May human behavior influence economic change? Is it possible that human behavior may bring the country social economic change in macro economic or micro behavioral economic view ? I shall indicate publishing industry example. Do you feel that if there are many students feel learning is very important when they read many books or many of students feel interesting to read or they have reading new books in habit, then it is possible that the country will have many students like to spend time to go to any book shops to choose the books, they feel that they can help they learn new knowledge. Then the country will increase students number, they often spend time to visit any one book shop every week. Their visiting book shops behavior which may become their habits. So, the country will increase students number, they often spend time to visit book shops. Also, it implies that visiting book shops behaviors may be their behavioral habits.

So, when the country has many students often spend time to visit book shops , their visiting book shops behaviors may help any one book shop to raise books sale chance. So, the country's student individual often visiting book shop behaviors, their habitual visiting book shops behaviors must may assist help any one book shop to increase books sale number absolutely.

Consequently, any one book shop , its books sale bumber must be influenced to increase to increase because the country will have many students like or feel need visit book shops habit in order to choose any suitable books to buy to read at home in order to raise themselves learning effort. When the country has many bok shops often have many students visit their book shops, then their books sale number may be influenced to increase. It explain why student individual visiting book shop behavior may help any one book shop sale number increases also.

How human productive behavior may influence economic development

May any country which citizen behavior assist themselves country development? It is one cause and effect economic question. I mean that if the country itself citicen can not concentrate mind or energy to choose to do one kind of industry in order to let themselves country can bring the most benefit, then whether the counry itself economy can bring the most serious economic benefit. I shall attempt to indicate these countries themselves indistry choice to explain whether these countries themselves citizen productive behavior may help themselves countries to achieve the largest economic benefits. I shall indicate as below:

New Zealand farmer individual wine productive behavior

For New Zealand country example, this country concerns itself effort is foucs on farming agricultural aspect. So, this country has many farmers concentrate on farming agricultural aspect. May New Zealanders choose to spend time to produce different kinds of wines, e.g. wine or red grape wine is for the people are eating meat, or they are eating dinner.

When these New Zealanders their behaviors choose to do farming or agriculture to grow and produce different kinds of taste of white or red grape wine drinking products job. Themselves grape agriculture behavior will influence these New Zealanders themselves, they can learn how to improve different kinds of grape wine drinking products in order to achieve every kinds of white or read grape wines taste improving aim during their white or red grape producing process.

Why can New Zealander every individual white or read grape wine producers improve their white or read grape wine taste more easily? In behavioral economic view, it can explain that why any one New Zealander white or read grape wine producer can be encouraged or excited or persuaded to concentrate nervous and energy and effort to learn how to improve their white or red grape wine products easily.

In fact, New Zealand is one agricultural food export country. It has good natural environment resource , e.g. land, seed to provide any one farmer to produce themselves any kinds of agricultrual food products, e.g. fruit, or wine food products. Because New Zealanders know themselves country has enough natural resource . So, in common, many New Zealanders choose to attempt to do farming agricultural jobs in order to export themselves any kinds of fruit or meat or wine products to overseas or sell to domestic in order to earn profit.

So, when these New Zealand farmers number has been increasing every year. This country farmers will feel themsleves competition between this

New Zealand farmers themselves are serious due to they may feel New Zealanders choose to do agriculture businesses in order to export themselves different kinds of farming food to overseas or sell to local to earn profit.

Hence, when many New Zealand farmers feel that farmers number has been increasing every year. They will feel themselves competition is serious. They must need to spend much time and nervous and effort to research what method is the best how to produce the best taste of white or red grape wine products in order to let local or overseas wine buyers to choose to buy his/her producing white or read grpae products to drink.

Hence, in competition psychological view, may influence many New Zealand white or reaad wine producers had been beginning to change their learning behavior on researching what method is the best in order to produce the best quality of taste red or white wine products to sell in order to attract overseas or local white or read grape wine drinkers to choose to buy his/her wine products. Their behavior will focus on learning how to raising or improving white or read grape wine taste method more than only focus on producing a large number white or red grape wine products. They believe wine quality is more important to compare wine producing number. So, New Zealand wine producers themselves wine producers behaviors have been changing on concentrating on researching wine quality method aspect more then wine producing number aspect in behavioral economic view.

America high technological productive behavior

For America example, US is one high technological country, it owns many high technological knowledge talent inventors, e.g. computer science inventors. Hence, US must attract many diferent countries owning high technological computer inventors choose to go to US to develop their computer science profession career. Also, it seems that when many computer science inventors or professions choose to go to US to develop themselves computer science new career. In behavioral economic view, due to their leaving themselves countries choice, which may bring influence themselve country job behaviors need to be changed. They must need to adapt US new live. Because they will forgive their past computer science job. These computer science professionals need to spend time to adapt US new lives. They " past computer science job behaviors" will need to be changed to their new US any computer employer's new computer science job model.

Because their traditional computer science jobs needed to be forgot in their themselves countries. They will feel their old computer science job knowledge and behavior needed to change in order to let their US any one new of computer company employer feels satisfactory to accept their new working behavior in any one US computer organization.

So, on the other hand, many US computer company employer will feel that they must need time to accept any one new overseas computer science professions their working behaviors, their working attitude daily, because these foreign comouter science professional, their past computer working behaviors and working attitude must be different to US domestic computer science professions.

In behavioral economic view, these overseas computer science professions, their working behaviors and attitude must be needed to change in order to adapt any one US new computer company itself domestic or local computer science professional stafs themselves daily working behaviors and attitude because these overseas and local computer science professionals must need to team work together.

In behavioral economic view, it is only one way that foreign computer science professionals must need to change themselves past country traditiona daily working behaviors and attitude in order to cooperate with these US local computer science professionals in teams more easily.

Consequently, if these foreign compute science professionals can change their past working behaviors and attitude to let any one US local computer science professional feels to cooperate with them easily in short time. Then, the US computer company itself whole computer professional teams themselves efficiencies will be influenced to raised or improved by the changing past working attitude and working behaviors of these foreign computer science professionals. So, in behavioral economic view, only if US any one computer company hopes itself computer teams themselves efficiency can be raised or improved when it decides to employ foreign computer science professionals and US domestic computer science professionals. They need to work in teams together. They must need to let these foreign computer science professionals to know how to change their working behaviors and attitude to let their domestic computer science professionals feel easy to work together. Then, the US computer company itself whole team efficiency must be rasied or improved easily in short time.

● China share market investing behavior

For China share market example, economic development depends on financial market. Because if many Chinese have interest to invest to carry on shares buying and selling activities in orde to learn how to earn shares interest and share profit when the China shareholder can make decision to sell himself/herself shares in the the high price, then he/she can earn money when he/she can sell the China company's shares in the high sale share price position.

If China has many Chinese like to spend time to carry on investing shares activities. Themselves shares buying and selling behaviors will influence China has many companies can increase fund from many Chinese shareholders in order to have enough money to expand or develop themselves businesses in China in long term.

Consequently, when China can have many Chinese like to attempt to carry on buying and selling shares investing behaviors in China share market. Themselves buying and selling shares behaviors can help many Chinese companies have effort to increase enough money or capital in order to continue to do their businesses in long term absolutely. So, it explains why when many Chinese become shareholders , they can assist China will have many companies continue to develop their businesses if many Chinese like to carry on shares buying and selling investing behaviors in long time in China financial investment market nowadays in behavioral economic view.

Why has any individual country have many people invest share behavior which can influence the country's macro consumption desire?

I shall apply shares market buying and selling investment behavior to explaiin why shares investment behavior which may impact the country's overal consumption desire as below:

In behavioral economic view, I assume that when the coutry has many people have interest to attempt to carry on shares buying and selling investment behavior, then their frequent shares buying and selling behaviors which may bring negactive consumption desire or shopping desire of these shares investors their consumer behavior.

The reason is simple, when the country has many share buyers number suddenly been increasing rapidly. Consequently, these large group share investors must need to spend much time to research any kinds of company shares variations, whether when their share prices will rise up of fall down in order to achieve buying the company's shares in the lowest price and selling the company's shares in the highest price level in order to earn profit.

Basic on this reason, they must need to spend much extra time to research share prices changing behavior every day, e.g. one working person will wait to leave his/her job, after he/she can spend time to gather data to research the day's share price changing behavior after dinner. So, the working person's right time may be his/her share price market research behavior. Before he/she may spend his/her night time to go to shopping after dinner, but nowadays, he/she will fogive to do his/her shopping behavior before dinner or after dinner at hight sometime. He/she will make decision to spend much night time to turn on computer to click on share market website to research his/her share purchase choice to investigate whether his/her share price whether it rises up or falls down at the moment in order to make his/her share buying or selling decision at ever night time.

I mean the when the country has many people are share investors, their shares investment behavioral spenging time which will influence many shops lose customers at might often because the country will have many people feel need to spend night time to turn on computer or watch television to investigate share price variation. So, the country will have many people / share investors choose to stay at home in order to carry on share price variation investigation behavior, they need to listen share market update news from radios or watch the share market update news from computer or TV at home every night. Consequenly, they must reduce times to leave themselves homes at night. So, their shopping behavior also will be reduced. Because these share investors feel need to spend time to investigate share price variation news at homes which can bring economic benefits (high opportunity benefits) when they choose to forgive to leave homes to go to shopping times (opportunity cost) every night.

On conclusion, it seems that when the country has many people are share investors, then their share price investigating behavior may bring negative shopping emotion at night. Consequently, the country's any one shop may lose many customers from this share investor consumer group in behavioral economic view. Hence, when the country's share investors number had been increasing rapidly, it will influence any shops lose many customers from this share investing customer group at night frequenly in short time, even long time in behavioral economic view, because their shopping desires or shopping emotion will be brought negative feeling when they make decisions to spend much time to listen radios or watch TV or computers share price update nes at night. Hence, share market will bring negative impact to influence consumer shopping desire or negative shopping emotion in behavioral economic view.

Can technology influence human shopping behavioral change?

Nowadays, technological development has reached mature stage, whether technological mature stage may bring positive or negative shopping emotion influence to global consumers. I shall aplly internet inventin or ecommerce shopping channel tool to explain whether internet technology can bring postive or negative influence to global consumer behavior in behavioral economic view.

Internet is a good technological tool, it brings e-commerce business chance. In fact, commonly, global has have many businessmen choose to use internet channel to carry on their products transactions between global online-buyers and their electronic websites. So, global many shoppers had begun to feel online shopping is more convenient to compare visiting shops shopping. Their shopping behaviors have been changed from internet technological tool. Global has many shoppers choose to buy any products from any overseas or local businessmen their web stores. They only need to spend time to find any businessmen their webstores to choose the most suitable products to pay visa to buy from their webstores. at homes. So, in general, global had have may shoppers had changed their shopping behaviors from visiting shops to visiting webstores at homes often.

So, it seems that internet technological tool had influenced global many shops disappear, but internet webstores will be replaced their actual shops on streets. Some of businessmen either they choose webstores to replace shops or choose websotes and shops both or still keep shops only. Hence, internet tool influences global businessmen have three kinds of products sale channels to let globa local and

overseas consumers to choose how to buy their products.

However, in fact, many of global shoppers, youngers and olders had begun to accept to buy any products from webstores. They feel to spend time to leave homes to visit shops , their shopping behaviors will be wasted time to not essential part to their daily lives. Hence, since internet technological invention, it had changed many consumers their traditional visiting shops shopping habit to change to buying products from webstores channel.

However, on the one hand, internet creates webstores ecommerce shopping channel to let global many consumers do not need to leave homes to go to shopping. It brings negative visiting shops shopping emotion to global general consumers nowadays. But on the other hand, it also brings positive visiting internet webstores shopping emotion to global general consumer nowadays. So, it seems that global many consumers feel that they often do not need to spend much time to go out shopping. Many global consumers feel convenient and enjoy to choose any products to buy from different internet webstores, when the online buyer chooses the most suitable product, he she only needs to pay visa card to buy the product from the online seller's webstore conveniently at home.

Hence, online shopping can bring economic benefit to online buyers, e.g. avoiding walking time or spending transport fare to visit the shop to go to shopping, shortening or reducing shopping time to do another important matter.

On conclusion, global many consumers began feel online shopping can bring more economic benefits on shortening shopping time, avoiding transport fare spending aspect. So, online shopping will be popular shopping behavior for future long time. It may encourage global many shoppers can make rapid shopping decision in short time in order to carry on any products buying transaction to global any one online shopper in short time easily in behavioral economic view. So, global many businessmen had begun to build themselves one attraction webstore in order to persuade different countries consumers to choose to click themselves webstores from internet channel to buy any kinds of products in short time easily.

So, internet technology had changed consumers traditional shopping behaviors to build positive online shopping emotion as well as raise online sellers' any products sale chance easily in behavioral economic view.

Why and how human behavior may influence the country's economic growth or recession?

When one country has many people choose to do the same matter for one period, whether their behavior may influence the country's pvera; economic growth or recession . I shall attempt to indicate cases toexplain their relationship as below:

For flowing rubblish behavioral case example, do you feel that when the country has many people often flow rubblish on the streets, instead of their flowing rubblish behavior may bring streets dirty? But, their flowing rubblish behavior may explain that this country has people may have enough money to buy food to ear, or enough cloths to wear, enough bottles of water to drink, even they may have enough money to buy new television, radio, refrigeraters , washing machines, desktops or laptops electronic home products from old to new to use in order to satisfy their living needs. So, when they flow old electronic home products, their flowing old home electronic products behaviors may seem that they have enough money to buy other new home electronic products to replace old home electronic products to use at homes.

However, it seems thaat this country ought have many people have jobs to do. So, many of them, they can easy to make purchase decison to flow any old home electronic products and buy any new home electronic products to use . Because this country has many people have jobs to do. So, they can often not use old home electonic products to become rubblishs to flow on streets after they had bought any kinds of new home electronic homes.

In fact, it also implies that this country's economy grows rapidly. So, many businesses can glow up rapdly. When they expanded their businesses, they must need to increase employees number in order to let they help themselves to raise productivity or serve their clients absolutely. So, when the country has many businesses can grow up, it seems that its economy must be better or it is improved to compare past. Due to many different kinds of home electronic products had been often bought to use by this country people in this period. So, this country's any streets can be observed that expensive electronic home products were flowed on streets anywhere. then, this country will have many electronic home products sellers can sell their home electronic products very easily. When this country has many people can find any kinds of jobs to do easily. So, due to unemploymen rate had been decreasing.

In behavioral economic view, as this many electronic home products rubblish country case, we can observe this country may have many people have jobs to do. So, consumption number has been increased long time. So, cheap food, or expensive home electronic products may be rubblish on any streets. This country's people , their flowing rubblish behaviors may be explained that many of people have enough jobs to do, so they have ability to buy any good taste food to eat or buy any kinds of expensive electronic home products to use. So, this country's economy may be improved for this long period. So, in behavioral economic view, when this country can have many electronic home products rubblishs are flowed on anywherer in streets frequently. It seems that this country will have many people have jobs to do, so it causes they often change old home electronic products or replaced them easily, when they have enough income to spend to buy any kinds of new home electronic products to use at homes easily. Moreover, their flowing old electronic home products behaviors also indicate that this country has many people their salaries may be increased in possible from their emplyers. When this country can have many different kinds of home electornic products are sold. It means that this country's electronic home products needs or demand had been increasing, due to many people have jobs to do and income increases to excite their living of needs also improve. Consequently, this country may seem have better economic improvement. We can observe from this country's electronic home products rubblish increasing income in theis period.

On conclusion, this country ought experience economic growth at this period. So, " flowing expensive electronic home rubblish increasing number " may seem that this country's economic growth is rapidly in this period, due to many people have jobs to do as well as salaries increase in this period.

Technology how impacts human behavior changing?

Technology how influences human behavior to bring changing? For example, online share purchase and sale transaction from smart phone brings share investor can do share buying or selling transation in any where and any time conveniently, non manual driving auto vehicle, bring car owner feels comfortable and spends free time to do other matter, e.g. reading, listening mucis in himself or herself car freely. electrical energy vehicle can help car owner to reduce air polluton and it can brings the drivers do not feel drive long time in any journeys in order to avoid air pollution for environmental protection responsible car drivers in our societies. Thus, they will drive long time in any journeys when they can drive electronic energy cars to replace oil energy cars.

However, online technology can also bring consumers can choose to stay at homes to buy any things from seller individual online webstore conveniently. Such as online technology can bring shoppers do not need to spend much time to visit shops to buy any things. They can choose any kinds of products from any online sellers individual online webstores conveniently at homes. Online technology excite busy consumers can make purchase decision easily as well as it can help online sellers sell any kinds of products from internet easily.

In behavioral economic view, technology can change human behavior to be improved, it can let human feels comfortable, more free time ro use, rapid making any decisions, such as apply smart phones to make share purchase or sale transaction decision, online shopping decision, even travelling any where decision in short time, when the traveller finds the most cheap hotel accommodation room price and air ticket price frm any travel agent online tourism webstore, then the potential travel customer can follow the online hotel accommodation price and air ticket price data to make decision when to buy the air ticket from the airline travel agent or make decision when to prebook which hotel accommodation room to go to the country to travel from online travel agent tourism webstores. So, technology can encourage global any country travelers to make anywhere to trvel rapidly. If the traveler can find the country's general hotel rooms and airline tickets prices had been decreasing more sightly. The traveler may make travel decision to choose the country to travel in short time, then he/she can prebook the country;s any hotel room and airline ticket to pay by visa fraom the country's any hotel and airline travel agent webstores., before one week, even one month or more easily. Hence, online technology can also encourage traveler individual frequent travel times to be increased, due to global travelers can find any hotel rooms and airline tickets prices from internet conveniently at homes. They do not need to spend time to visit any airline travel agent to enquire travel choice country's hotel rooms prices and airline ticket prices. They can compare global travel of countries choices ' all hotels rooms and airline agents air tickets prices to make prebook airline seat and hotel room decision before one week, one month even six months early.

On conclusion, online technology can encourage global travelers can make travelling any where and when traveling time desicions easily. It can excite tourism industry develops in long time. Also, such as electricity cars invention can encourage environment protection car owners do car purchase decision easily, because they can choose to drive electronic energy cars to replace oil energy cars in order to avoid air pollution occurs easily. So, electronic cars can increase electronic car purchasrs number, due to many of environmental protection attitude of car owners can choose to drive electricity cars to bring air cleans, even non -manual driving cars can encourage lazy driving and free time driving car owners to choose to buy non-manual (artificial intelligent) cars to drive , because they can spend much free time to read, listen music or do any matters in themselves cars, they do not need to drive cars, robotic (AI) auto driving machine is such one non-manual driver to help them to drive themselves cars confidently. So, non-manual driving cars can attract lazy and enjoying free time driving car owners to choose to buy to replace traditional manual cars to drive easily. Moreover, online share transaction can help any share investors to make share buying and selling decision in short time easily. When they can apply smart phones technological tool to carry on share buying and selling activities easily. They can observe any share rising or falling price suitation from smart phones in any where any any time easily. So, smart phone technology can help global any shareholders to make share purchase and sale transaction easily. So, technology can encourage human makes decision in short time rapidly.

How and why employees behaviors may influence economy development?

In behavioral economy view,I believe the country's any organizational employees behavior may bring indirect relationship to influence the country's long term economic development. I shall indicate past manufacture industry social development period to explain their relationship. For many countries' past business activities had belonged to manufacturing industry, such as US, UK past before 1980 year, it focused on steel manufacturing and steel manufacturing related machine products. So, US, Uk developed countries manufacturing industries may be past main country's economic income sources. I assume US , UK past had one million number different kinds of industries. They ought had about seven houndred thousand number organizational businesses were belonged to manufactured industry. They may include:
Steel manufacturing and steel related machine manufacturing, e.g. vehicle manufacturing, home appliances, e.g. washing machine, television, radio, refrigerate cooler, heater, air condition etc. different kinds of different kinds of steel -related manufacturing machine, they were manufactured from US, UK steel machine manufacturers. So, US, Uk the other three hundred thousand number industry may be general service industry, e.g. hotel service, restaurent, cinema, public transport service, tourism lesiure , wine bar, supermarket etc. different kinds of non-manufacturing industries business organizations were operated in UK, US past before 1980 year.
So, in UK, US developed countries industry development history, they ought have high percentage of businesses belonged to steel related manufacturing machine and steel products. Also, in the past before 1980 year, US, Uk business employers , they employed many workers are manufacturing workers. They needed to spend long time to work in factories. They were skillful workers, and they are trained to manufacturing cars, washing machine, television, heater, etc. even steel itself different kinds of steel related products to prepare to deliver to their shops to sell to US, Uk local or overseas clients.

So, I believe that past UK, US ought employ many employees, they belonged to skillful manufacturing workers, manufacture increasing steel machine or steel related machine number of products rapidly daily. So, if UK, US had had many of these manufacturing factories owned high skillful workers, then their manufacturing steel-related machine or steel both kinds of products number must be influenced to raise rapidly. Consequently, their steel machine manufacturing products would been exported to overseas or would been sold to local both markets , they may be influenced to raise sale number. They (these manufacturing workers) needed to be trained to know how to manufactur these different kinds of machine products in the efficient teams and they ought to be trained to raise their efficiencies in order to shorten time to manufacturing many kinds of steel related manufacturing machine or steel itself products rapidly. So , if their efficiencies and manufacturing performance was improved, these US, UK any one manufacturing worker and their teams ought achieve raising productivities significantly.

Hence, when past UK, US manufacturing industry development period, if these two countries' any manufacturing factories could have many manufacturing workers could be trained to be skillful and proficient manufacturing workers. Then, in past every day to these factories workers, they ought help their steel or steel related manufacturing employers to raise any kinds of machine or steel products number in every team. So, when past in the manufacturing industry development, US, UK could have many factories' manufacturing workers themselves steel or steel related machine products manufacturing skill could be trained to to improve to any kinds of these machine or steel manufacuring products quality as well as their products number could be influenced to raise by themselves skillful improvement significantly every day.

Then, what would be influenced to occur to past UK, US manufacturing industry period? In behavioral economic view, when these two manufacturing industry developed countries, such as UK, US , if they had many factories workers can be trained to improve their skill in order to achieve any kinds of steel or steel-related machine products quality could be improved as well as products manufacturing number could be also increased absolutely.

In consequence, past UK and US both countries ought increase themselves any kinds of steel and steel related machine products number to be supplied to themselves local shops to let local clients to choose any one kind of machine manufacturing products to buy easily as well as they could also export to supply overseas any countries to buy their different kinds of steel or steel related machine products to let overseas steel or steel related manufacturing machine product buyers, they can have many of these different kinds of these steel or steel-related different kinds of manufacturing machine from UK and UK these both countries easily to compare other countries.

On conclusion, I believe that past US, and UK macro manufacturing industry income GDP would increase significantly. So, they would have good economic growth performance because when many of these manufacturing workers themselves manufacturing effort could be improved. So, it explained when employees manufacturing abilities can influence economic growth indirectly.

Robots invention whether they can help organizations to raise efficiencies or inefficiencies?

In behavioral economic view, in any organizations, when the organization hopes its worker teams can raise efficiencies , the organization may choose to increase more workers number and/or it can provide training to improve these workets themselves skills in order to raise their efficiencies. For one warehouse example, when the warehouse increases many goods , they are needed to delivered these goods from the shelves to the delivering destination locations. If this warehouse supervisors feel these workers themselves goods delivery speeds are slow, which is possible due to this warehouse's workers number is not enough. So, this warehouse supervisor ought increase workers number in order to increase their goods delivery speed in order to deliver goods from the shelves to every indicated goods delivery destination in order to let any one lorry driver can transport the right kinds of goods and ensure the accurate goods number to transport to any one client home rapidly.

However, if this warehouse supervisor planed to buy several warehouse goods delivery robots to assist these warehouse workers to find the right kinds of goods from shelves and then deliver to the right destination location in the warehouse. So, these warehouse orkers can concentrate on counting the accurate goods number and ensuring the right kinds of goods in order to prepare to let lorry drivers to transport these goods to these goods of buyers themselvers homes rapidly. Consequently, in the first step, robots can concentrate on finding th right goods from shelves and delivers them to the right goods transportation of location destination.

Then, in the second step, these warehouse workers can concentrate on counting the accurate goods number and ensuring the right kinds of goods in order to prepare to put them to the lorry. Consequently, when warehouse robots and warehouse workers can cooperate to work together, the most important, robots, can deal on finding the right kinds of goods and deal on delivering the accurate number of goods of job duty as well as these warehouse workers can only concentrte on counting the right kinds of goods number in order to avoid it has none any mistake of wrong kinds of goods and inaccurate goods of delivery number to be transported to the lorry and to deliver to any one buyer's home.

So, it seems that warehouse robots ought help any one warehouse worker to raise himself efficiency and avoid goods delivery of mistake occurrence easily as well as their help to warehouse workers that can let any one goods buyer feels their goods can be delivered to their homes rapidly. Moreover, warehouse robots can also help these warehouse workers to raise efficiencies because warehouse robots can help them to shorten goods delivery time between any one shelf and any one goods delivery destination of location in the warehuse because robots may help them to find the right kinds of goods from the right shelf in the short time. So, any one worker does not need to spend long time to seek anywhere is the right shelf location for the kind of goods when the kind of goods are needed to deliver to the buyer's home from lorry. Warehouse robots can help them to do this aspect of " finding the goods from the right shelf in short time job duty". So, any one warehouse worker only needed tospend less time to do the counting of any right kind of goods number and ensuring the right kind of goods job duty. Consequently, this warehouse 's any one worker, his any one kind of goods delivery time may be reduced, because robots' assistance and they may have more confidence to avoid mistake to deliver the wrong number of goods and/or the wrong kind of goods to any one goods buyer's home.

On conclusion, it seems that warehouse robots ought may help any one warehouse worker to raise efficiency for any one team in the warehouse as well as the warehouse any one supervisor does not need to spend much time to observe any one worker individual performance for " goods delivery job duty aspect" because their goods delivery job duty that had been replaced to do by these several warehouse robots. Robots can achieve the more accurate of right kinds of goods and the right number of goods delviery job performance to compare any one of human warehouse worker themselves right kinds of goods of delivery and right number of goods of delivery job performance. So, when robots can participate to cooperate with this warehouse's any one worker to do their goods of delivery job duty in this warehouse every day. Then, robots can raies any one of supervisor individual confidence in order to let they do not need to spend time to observe any one of worker individual whose goods of delivery job performane. They can concentrate on supervising any one worker whose goods transport to lorry in the final step in order to avoid to deliver wrong goods number and / or wrong kind of goods to any one goods buyer's home every day. Consequently, this warehouse's overall teams of their delviery of goods performance many be improved by robotss' participatin to goods of delivery task as well as this warehouse's oveall teams themselves efficiencies may be influenced to raise by robots' goods of delivery task participation.

Why social behavior may influence organizational strategy needs to be changed ?

Why any organizations need to know whether nowadays social behaivor how has been changing in order to implement the kind of the most right strategy to achieve the profit aim pursue in possible. I shall indicate nowadays ecommerce or online, customer shopping behavior to explain above question concerns they ought have close relationship between social behavior and organizational strategic choice or organizational behavioral changing need.

On nowadays ecommerce business, or online shopping model, this kind of shopping model in global many young and old age consumers like to apply internet tool to choose any country sellers website stores in order to stay at home to buy any kinds of products from themselves webstores in global societies.

In fact, online shopping model had been popular for long time above to twenty years. Most of global sellers will make decision to design themselves webstores in order to attract global many online buyers to choose to buy their products from themselves webstores. So, it seems that social consumers purchase behaviors had been changed to online shopping from internet invention.

Hence, social consumers purchase behavioral changes may influence any organizations' strategies need to be changed from visiting shops purchase strategy model to online purchase strategy model, if the seller still concentrate on concentrate on considerate how to design itelf , but neglects to considerate how to design itself webstore, e.g. how to design attract product photos to put on itself webstore, how to arrange sale price information location to be putted on webstore and visa card payment location on itself webstore in order to let any one online buyer can feel very easier to buy itself any kinds of products from itself webstore. Then, its potential online buyers will be influenced to increase number when they can find this online seller itself any kinds of products photes and every kinds of product sale price information and visa card payment channel locations easily from itself webstore.

So, it implies that nowadays any one seller ought need to design one webstore to let any one online overseas and domestic consumers can have chance to click itself webstore to choose any one kind of product to buy conveniently when he/she does not hope to leave him/her home to go to shop, because nowadays social shopping behaviors had been influenced to change when internet invention, them it gives another online purchase method to replace visiting shops purchase method to global any one buyer in nowadays societies.

So, if nowadays any one seller still concentrate on how to design itself shop display in order to put any kinds of product on shelf in order to let any one visiting shop customer to find the kind of product to buy, but it neglects to change to choose to pursue another new technological shopping method, such as webstore purchase method in order to implement effective strategy to design the most right webstore as well as in order to attract global overseas and local consumers to find itself webstore easily from website and find its any one kind of product phots and sale price and visa card payment button in order to choose to buy itself any kinds of products in the short time. Consequently I believe that the seller will lose many customers from overseas and local when its other same or similar product sellers choose to design themselves webstores in order to let global any one product buyer can buy themselves any one kind of product when they can pay visa card to buy their products from them webstores conveniently when they stay at home habitly. Then, the seller will lose many global potential customers in long time.

On conclusion, in behavioral economic view, any consumer behavioral social changing, which will influence any in order to avoid customers number loses significantly . In future time, organizations need to make rapid decision in order to implement the most reasonable and the most useful strategy in order to avoid global potential customers number reduces or lose them in long time. So, social behavioral changing environment ought influence any global organizations need to decide how to change themselves strategies in order to avoid customers loses significantly in future time.

155